ALSO BY DIANA ATHILL

Fiction
*Don't Look at Me Like That*

Memoirs
*After a Funeral*
*Make Believe*

# LIFE CLASS

# LIFE CLASS

The Selected Memoirs
of Diana Athill

GRANTA

Gr                           11 4QR

This book                                *terday Morning*,
first publ                              blished 2003;
*Instead of*                            , published by
Robin Cla                           st published by
Granta Boo                      *vhere Towards the*
*End*, first pu                          . published 2009.

A CIP catalogue record for this book
is available from the British Library.

1 3 5 7 9 10 8 6 4 2

ISBN 978 1 84708 123 0

Printed and bound in Great Britain by
MPG Books Ltd, Bodmin, Cornwall

# Contents

# INTRODUCTION

In the early 1980s, the publisher André Deutsch had an idea for a book I could write about the partition of India. I didn't take it up, which I regret now because it was a good suggestion and I was wrong to imagine, as I told him, that 'everything' had already been written about the subject. Instead, I proposed a thought of my own: a book about Indian railways, part travel account, part technical history and part family memoir. Too *many* parts, clearly, but André liked the idea and a few weeks later I went to his office, where he took out a fountain pen and ceremonially wrote a cheque, saying words to the effect that this was his happiest moment since the day he thought he'd signed up George Orwell (as I guess he told many writers of first books) and then stealing a cigarette from my packet to smoke in celebration.

I went to India for a year and did too much research. There was certainly a lot to find out, but the finding out eventually became a way of postponing the writing. Soon after I came home to London, Mrs Gandhi was assassinated in Delhi, which meant there was further postponement as I turned back to journalism. Then one day the phone rang and it was André, wondering how the book was 'coming along'. The truth was that it wasn't coming along, but I wrote two short chapters in a panic and sent them in as evidence that his money hadn't gone completely to waste. André's response was to invite me to his office for lunch. It was there that I met a brisk woman in glasses, who told me that what I had written was very good and then read a page or two of it aloud to us: to André, perhaps because he had never bothered to read it himself (the thought occurred to me only later), and to me perhaps to persuade me that what I'd written was as good as she said, and the book worth persevering with.

She had a fine voice, precise and low, of the kind many more people had then than now, though even in 1984 her kind of accent had lost its claim to be the English that the nicest and best people spoke. 'Patrician', 'RP' and 'Oxbridge' would be the easy adjectives, though what it reminded me of was listening to the BBC's Home Service as a boy and watching British films of the same period where pretty well everyone spoke like this other than junior policemen and Cockney chars in pinafores. No matter. She read aloud – a few hundred words about an old-fashioned grocer's shop in an Indian railway town – and the fact was that her voice's elegance and intelligence seemed to elevate what I'd written, just as words scribbled in ballpoint seem profoundly transformed when set in twelve-point Baskerville. There may have been an almost maternal element to her encouragement. She certainly had something of the kindly schoolmistress or university tutor about her: her thick-framed glasses, her enthusiasm, her opinion that I simply *had* to go on with it otherwise I'd be letting myself down. As life turned out, I didn't go on with it; I went back to newspapers and returned André's advance, and therefore as an illustration of Diana Athill's persuasive editorial technique my story is unsatisfactory, showing nothing more than how my torpor, fear and the need to make money could defeat one of the finest minds in British publishing. All I know is that if anyone could have drawn that book out of me it would have been her.

Diana would have been sixty-six then. She had been André's right-hand woman for nearly forty years and went on serving the company that bore his name, even after André had left it, for another eight. André was the entrepreneurial spirit behind the enterprise but it was mainly Diana who developed its reputation for good books by finding and fostering writers such as Jean Rhys and V.S. Naipaul. The story of her long professional life as an editor is brilliantly told in *Stet*, the second book in this anthology, and there's no need to add to it here. What I didn't know when I met her was that she was also a writer; or rather *had been* a writer, because her most recent book had been published nearly twenty years before. Few people remembered her novel (*Don't Look at Me Like That*, 1967) or her story collection (*An Unavoidable Delay*, 1962), which found a publisher in the USA but none in Britain. It was the middle book of her small 1960s oeuvre that knowledgeable readers, particularly women, mentioned when I said that I'd met her. 'Oh, but you must read *Instead of a Letter*,' they said. The book wasn't easy to find. It had been republished a few times since it first appeared in 1962 and probably was more often in print than out of it, but by the early 1980s *Instead of a Letter* was more of a cult than the popular classic it deserved to be. The times weren't right. Literary taste was still largely dictated by male sensibilities, and, while feminist publishing in Britain had begun to thrive, Athill didn't quite fit its political agenda. As to the book's form, 'memoir' had yet to be established as a successful category in bookshops. Writers wrote them, of course, but rarely did they become known for the memoir alone (J.R. Ackerley and Laurie Lee may be two exceptions). Publishers and readers thought instead of 'autobiographies', in which intimate personal disclosure took a back seat to records of achievement. The boundary between the two forms is blurred and bridgeable: V.S. Pritchett's wonderful account of his early life, *A Cab at the Door*, was described as 'autobiography' when it first appeared in 1968, whereas now it would have 'memoir' written all over it. Gore Vidal explained the difference in this way: 'A memoir is how one remembers one's own life, while an autobiography is history, requiring research, dates, facts double-checked'. His statement is arguable, but it has the virtue of simplicity. More important, by stressing subjective, unverified memory it permits the memoirist to misremember and, unconsciously or otherwise, to embroider and invent – an indulgence, it has to be said, that Diana Athill has never been interested to take.

At any rate, I got *Instead of a Letter* from the library. It told

Diana's story from birth to the age of forty-two, a life begun idyllically in the English countryside, a life rich with privilege and promise – horses, sailing, books, an Oxford education – until, aged twenty-two, she is jilted by her fiancé and her dreams of a future as an RAF pilot's wife turn to dust. Happiness vanishes for the next twenty years. Rejection destroys her confidence, especially in her relationships with men, and she regains it fully only in early middle age, not through the once hoped-for avenues of marriage and children but when she begins to write and has a story published in a newspaper. Put like that it seems an ordinary enough progression – happy, then unhappy, then happy enough – and perhaps an advertisement for a creative-writing school (*'Miserable? Jilted? Then learn to write the Miss Lonelyhearts way!'*). But at that time I had never read a book like it, and to my mind only a few memoirs have equalled it since.

The most memorable and pleasing aspect of memoirs often comes from the picture they offer of a character or a period. We remember V.S. Pritchett's rackety father besotted by Christian Science and mistresses, or John McGahern's loving mother walking her son through the lanes of County Leitrim, or Blake Morrison's father bluffing his Yorkshire way out of and into trouble. The writer attends as a witness, but his own selfhood – what he was like – is present at most as an interlocutor of the character of others. Direct self-description is one of the hardest tasks a writer can undertake, because self-knowledge is so difficult and because the risks of self-indulgence, self-dramatization and falsity of all kinds are so great (and easily spotted and mocked). Diana's book was certainly about herself, and the core of it about the severe disappointment that altered, and for a long time deadened, the course of her life. In other hands, it could have been a long wallow with an unconvincingly bright little salvation at the end. Many books are now constructed on this principle: look, I was an addict; behold, my suffering when I was abused. Often the authors say their motive is to give consolation and hope to others in the same position. *Instead of a Letter* certainly had this effect. About a hundred readers (ninety-nine of them women) wrote to her after the book was first published to share their experience and say how much comfort the book had provided – a large response to an unknown writer when authorship was much less publicized than it is now, and when communication involved the trouble of taking out pen and paper and buying a stamp. To be jilted, to have one's engagement broken off, left a public as well as a private scar (I remember the hush around the subject when in the 1950s it happened to an older cousin of mine). The distress caused by rejection may well be a historical constant in human beings, but at least since 1962 our more open and casual attitudes towards sex and marriage mean that the humiliation is no longer so deep. 'Guilt never caused me any serious distress, but humiliation did,' Diana writes in this anthology's third book, *Yesterday Morning*. 'Humiliation . . . was the sharpest misery I knew.'

An instructive story of self-help wasn't, however, what she intended by *Instead of a Letter*, nor is it by any means the book's most important attraction. Like thousands of other readers before and since, what held me about the writing was its candour. The quality has since become an Athill trademark, though in itself candour is no guarantee of literary pleasure or interest: frank books aren't always good books and can often be tedious by boasting of their frankness. Athill's way of being candid is more subtle and its effect more persuasive. The reader feels that what he is reading is as true a portrait of the writer and her experience as any words on paper can achieve. Part of this comes from her considerable gift as a maker of sentences, which are so lucid and direct; some of it is owed to the breaking of taboos that then surrounded female sexual behaviour; most of it, though, stems from her triumphant struggle to 'get it right', a lesson she learned from two of the writers she edited. Jean Rhys told her that the trick of good writing was 'to get it as it was, as it really was'. Vidia Naipaul said that 'provided you really get it right, the reader will understand'.

All feeling and experience occur inside specific contexts – a room, a field, a conversation, a country house, a crowded pub – and by getting these things 'right', as a good novelist might, Diana opened up what could have been a narrow story of injury and self-absorption into a book that takes pleasure in the world. Also, the harder thing, she got herself right by letting us see how she appeared to others. A chilling moment comes in *Instead of a Letter* when, soon after her engagement has been broken off, she reads a passage in her younger sister's diary. Her sister had a boyfriend who would hold her hand but refused to kiss her, though she was 'dizzy with expectation' that he might. This, remember, was early 1940. Diana read her diary entry: 'He told me that he was not going to kiss me though he wanted to. He said that I was going to be a fascinating woman but that I mustn't begin that sort of thing too soon or it would spoil me. *Look at Di, he said, you don't want to be like her. And of course I don't.*' More than twenty years later, Diana wrote that 'the shrivelling sensation of reading those words is something I still flinch from recalling'. She saw with a 'shameful, accepting humility . . . that I *was* diseased in other people's eyes: that unhappiness was not a misfortune but a taint. In the depths of my being I must have wanted to kill my sister for it, but all I recognised was a shuddering acknowledgment that out of the mouths of babes . . .' She then decided that she would be a model sister to her sibling, rejoicing at her triumphs and fretting over her sorrows. 'But there was a streak of falsity in it: I was over-compensating for my resentment at the scar she had left with her innocent, idle thrust.'

In a first-person narrative, someone else's diary can offer a useful change in the point of view. Another diary crops up in Diana's second memoir, *After a Funeral*, which was published in 1986. The book – Diana preferred to call it a 'documentary' – recounts the tragic story of 'Didi', a promising writer from Egypt who went to stay with Diana as her lodger after she befriended him as his publisher ('Didi' was in fact Waguih Ghali, whose novel *Beer in the Snooker Club* was published by Deutsch in 1964.) Their relationship becomes difficult and, on his part, bitter. Sex isn't the issue. Diana has a partner, called Luke in the book, and though she begins by wanting Didi she has sex with him only once, when both of them are drunk. One evening she goes into Didi's room and finds that he has left his diary open on his desk. She reads:

I have started to detest her. I find her unbearable . . . my reactions
to Diana are sparked by my physical antipathy to Diana. I find
it impossible to live in the same flat as someone whose physical
body seems to provoke mine to cringe. This has led me to detest
everything she does, says or writes . . . I'd be sitting in my
room watching a stupid thing on telly and annoyed with myself
for not switching it off and working . . . In her sitting-room her
typewriter would go tick tick tick tick tick. 'Christ,' I'd tell myself,
'there she is, hammering away at that bloody mediocre muck –
dishing out one tedious stupid sentence after another, and thinking –
no, *pretending* it is writing.

To quote such a passage about oneself in a book by oneself
takes . . . what? Courage certainly, but also an unusually strong
sense of duty towards the truth and the usefulness of truth to
literature. In *Yesterday Morning* she writes that the damage lies do –
the context is the anti-Catholic prejudices of her grandfather – may
be 'the central reason for trying to write the truth, even if indecent,
about oneself.' That may be the moral reason, but there is also a
literary one: Rhys's 'to get it as it was, as it really was'. She exposes
for all to see her pragmatic code of personal behaviour. Private
diaries left lying around invite themselves to be read; married
men can be fucked so long as nobody finds out (or worse, confesses)
and the harmony of the marital home is kept intact. This is the
way she was – as probably many of us are and will go on being.
The consequence is that Diana in her books doesn't always come
across as the most likeable of women. When Didi in his diary
notes that she pronounces 'spritzer' as 'SpritzA!' – Colonel Blimp
speaking – the reader may feel a certain sympathy with his
antagonism, even though accents are harmless accidents of birth.
But if she were more likeable, would she be more sympathetic – or
as believable?

The qualities that come with being a writer of Diana's sort aren't
always attractive. After she and Didi have their drunken sex, Didi
comes into the kitchen the next day and pleads with her not to tell
her lover.

'Promise me one thing. Promise that this is one thing you'll never tell Luke about.'

'Of course I won't, I promise.' (I was already mulling in my head the written account, as exact as possible, which I was going to show Luke one day.)

Graham Greene's famous dictum about the 'chip of ice' that lurks in every writer's heart has never had a better illustration. It would be hopelessly wrong, however, to think of Diana as all ice: a cold-eyed writing machine. The reason that we can read Didi's diaries and letters is that he left them to her in a letter in which he described her as the person he loved most. Then he killed himself, despite her enormous kindness to him, in his rent-free room in the flat where more than forty years later, as I write this, she still lives.

Recently I went to see her there. The flat is on the top floor of the last house in a Victorian cul-de-sac that ends in the green open spaces of Primrose Hill and has a fine view south across central London. Her cousin, the journalist Barbara Smith, owns the house and keeps an apartment on the ground floor; they have had this arrangement for half Diana's life, but when I visited her, in March 2009, Diana was making plans to move into a residential home for old people while she still had all her wits about her and could save friends and relations the trouble of making decisions on her behalf. Three months before, she had turned ninety-one. When a person is that age the present tense is safest deployed with fingers crossed, though there are very few signs of serious failing. She has a hearing aid and walks with the aid of a handsome silver-topped stick and uses a stair-lift to take her up (but not down) the four flights to her flat, but she still drives her little car and her conversation is as witty and direct as ever. She looks majestic.

As Diana's former publisher, I edited three of the four books that make up this collection. Very little needs to be said about that. The typescript arrived, a few suggestions for changes were made, Diana absorbed them with her quick editorial brain, and a slightly amended typescript was soon in the post. Editing her was pure

pleasure because I loved reading her; it was like having someone
speak into your ear, someone humane and self-amused and wise
that you wanted to hear. 'Good writing' is difficult to define, and
definitions differ according to taste, but you know it when you see
it, which is rarer than publishing companies would have you
suppose. I remember my excitement when I read the first few
pages of the typescript that became *Somewhere Towards the End*
(Diana's choice of title and a good one, as her titles always are).
The book arose out of a brief conversation and the exchange of a
postcard or two: it seemed to me that while the memoir genre
abounded in accounts of youth – the 'coming-of-age narrative' is
a literary cliché of our times – very few books have let us know
about life at the other end of the road. In fact, other than self-help
guides (take a cod-liver oil capsule every day) and the late novels
of Philip Roth, I could think of none. There are, of course, books
about the process of dying by victims of cruel and slow terminal
disease, but writers have been shy of the subject of *just being old*, as
if shame and indignity had replaced wisdom and experience as the
best-known qualities of great age. Our conversation hardly
amounted to an editorial briefing and I had no word of progress for
a couple of years. Then a few early pages arrived and with them the
first vivid sense of what it is like to become old, like reports from
another country that we shall all, if spared earlier elimination,
shortly be moving to. In different hands, the book could have been
filled with a sentimental longing for the past, brittle cheer towards
the present, or the religious consolation of the future. None of those
things could ever have appealed to Diana. Instead, *Somewhere
Towards the End* is a beautifully turned series of episodes, none of
them sermonic, in which the author reveals how she has come to
terms (or not) with what she calls 'falling away' and the unavoidable
fact of death. It was, wrote the late Simon Gray – no stranger
himself to intimations of mortality – both 'exhilarating and
comforting' in its good sense, candour and lively spirit. Every
passage is rooted in specifics. On the second page, she describes
her new tree fern (£18 from the Thompson & Morgan plant
catalogue) and her doubts that she will live long enough to see it

reach mature height: a small thought, but it immediately takes us inside the mind of someone going on for ninety. She has 'got it right', and continues to get it right throughout the book, in the sense that we utterly believe that this is how life is and was for her. She describes her final lover, Sam:

> We rarely did anything together except make ourselves a pleasant little supper and go to bed, because we had very little in common apart from liking sex . . . We also shared painful feet, which was almost as important as liking sex, because when you start feeling your age it is comforting to be with someone in the same condition. You recognize it in each other, but there is no need to go on about it. We never mentioned our feet, just kicked our shoes off as soon as we could.

*Stet, Yesterday Morning, Somewhere Towards the End*: they may not be her last books – fingers crossed again – but they represent the late flowering of a writing career previously conducted in sporadic bursts. All were written when she was in her eighties and all are memoirs. Sometimes they overlap; they weren't planned as a sequence. A few places and people in them wear a light disguise; when Diana began to write, it wasn't done to name names in intimate personal histories. Now it seems reasonable to name two of them, because of the important part they played in shaping her life.

The first is a place. 'Beckton', the country house and estate where Diana spent so much of her childhood, is in fact Ditchingham Hall in Norfolk, just across the river Waveney from Suffolk. Her mother's grandfather, a Yorkshire doctor enriched by railway shares and a good marriage, bought it in the 1890s. A cousin of hers still lives there. (Diana herself is far from well off. Publishing never paid her much, partly owing to her indifference about asking for more, which she came to see 'as foolish, if not reprehensible', and she had no inheritance. Having no money, Diana finds it easy to talk about. The royalties from her greatest success, *Somewhere Towards the End* will pay for her stay in the old people's home, somewhere closer towards the end. )

The second is a person. 'Paul', the young pilot who broke her heart, was Tony Irvine. As squadron leader A.T. Irvine he died in the late afternoon of April 13, Easter Sunday, 1941, when his Blenheim bomber crashed into a mountain near the village of Vigla in northern Greece. Germany had just begun its invasion of Greece and a squadron of seven Blenheims set out to bomb troop formations before they poured south through the Monastir Gap. German fighters attacked the Blenheims ('dreadful, clumsy planes' in Diana's recollection) and six were shot down in the space of four minutes. Irvine's plane was last seen climbing into the mist that surrounded the mountainside, possibly trying to escape. The following day its wreckage was found eighty-four feet below the peak. Irvine had married by that time and his wife was pregnant with a son. When Irvine's father died, long after, this son found a letter from Diana among his possessions and got in touch with her. They met one or twice. He must now be a man in his late sixties.

'Just say,' I said to Diana, 'that Paul hadn't jilted you, that you'd married him. Would you have written a book?'

Her reply was quick but thoughtful. 'If I'd been an air force wife, I probably wouldn't have written a book. If I'd been an air force widow, I might have done.'

In any event, a long time passed before she started on the book that became *Instead of a Letter*. She said she had no intention of writing it, no premeditation, no structure, no model presented by the books of other writers. 'That book *happened to me*,' she said, meaning that it had somehow taken charge of her and couldn't be stopped. She had written nine stories for her collection and begun a tenth. 'It was going to be about my grandmother but it fizzled out and I put it away. Then I took it out again and it simply *went on*. I couldn't stop. I wrote it even in the office in any spare moment. There was no plan and it's remained for me a very baffling book, but it worked as a piece of therapy to a quite extraordinary extent.'

She realized she could write, and that she was best at it when not covering reality with the polite wallpaper of fiction but by recounting experience as it really had been, as honestly as she could evoke it to her own satisfaction: 'I've never actually planned a book,' she said. 'I've never thought of readers.' In the forty-seven years since, only six books have followed, which brings her total to eight. She said, 'I've never written anything unless I've wanted to. I really am an amateur.'

I thought of her self-description – 'amateur' – as I went down the stairs and began to walk across Primrose Hill. Really, we should have more of them. More people who write only when they feel they have something to tell us; more writers driven by the scrupulous need to make us see clearly and exactly what they have witnessed and felt.

I walked on over the rise. London was now spread all across the horizon in its familiar jumble of offices and monuments. I thought of how Diana was born somewhere off to the right in Kensington during a Zeppelin raid (December 21, 1917) and of how she had seen this city in so many different ages and moods. In *Instead of a Letter*, she and Paul take a ride in London's last hansom cab – before the war and before her humiliating rejection. Before The Fall, you might say sadly, until you remember how Diana rose from it to find her singular voice. If anyone in future wants to know how an intelligent Englishwoman led her life in the twentieth century, her inner and outer life, from birth to a very old age, hers are books that will need to be read. As for now, they can simply be enjoyed.

*Ian Jack*
*May 2009*

# YESTERDAY MORNING

*Diana Athill with her mother, 1918*

# NOW

'OH MY GOD,' said my mother. 'Can I really have a daughter who is seventy?' and we both burst out laughing.

She was ninety-two. It was eight years since she had driven a car, six since social services had supplied her with a seat to help her bathe without getting stuck in the tub. She needed two sticks when she made her daily inspection of her garden, and had given up the needlepoint embroidery she loved because her sight was no longer good enough. She was well aware of being a very old woman, but she still felt like the Kitty Athill she had always been, so it was *absurd* to have another old woman as a daughter.

Another person, however, might have forgotten her own name before reaching that age, so it is impossible to generalize about growing old. Why, I was once asked, do so few people send back reports about life out on that frontier; and the answer is that some no longer have the ability because they have lost their wits, some no longer have the energy because they are beset by aches and pains and ailments, and those lucky enough to have hung on to their health feel just like they felt before they were old except for not being able to do an increasing number of things, and for an awareness of their bodies as sources of a slight malaise, often forgettable but always there if they think about it.

I belong to the last group, touch wood (once you have made it into your eighties you don't say something like that without glancing nervously over your shoulder). The main things I can no longer do are drink alcohol, walk fast or far, enjoy music, and make love. Hideous deprivations, you might think – indeed, if someone had listed them twenty years ago I would have been too appalled to go on reading, so I must quickly add that they are less hideous than they sound.

Drink, for instance: I did not have to say to myself 'Drink is no longer good for me *so I must give it up*'. What happened was that I began to wake up in the night quite often with a horrid pain which got worse and worse until I threw up, and eventually concluded that what caused this unpleasantness was alcohol. I took a long time to get there because often I had drunk no more than one or two glasses of wine with dinner, and who would suppose that one or two glasses of wine could make one ill? But they did, and by the time I understood as much, I was so tired of all that miserable sickness that I said goodbye to alcohol quite happily and began positively to enjoy water.

Being bad at walking is tiresome, but not so tiresome for me as it would be for some. In my youth I never walked where I could ride a horse, and later never where I could drive a car, which I can still do. My happiest times have been spent in chairs or beds: possibly I would actually like it if I became wheelchair-bound.

The loss of pleasure in music because of increasing deafness is sadder. The sounds can still be heard, but are distorted into ugliness. The piano comes through almost unaltered, but strings and birdsong are scratchy and painful, while most high voices are squawks. But against that, silence, like pure cold water, has become lovely.

As for sex – some very old women say that it still gives them pleasure, so clearly it varies from person to person. With me its ebbing was the first of the physical indications of old age: my body began slowly to lose responsiveness in my sixties, long before my mind did. For a while it could be restored by novelty, which allowed me an enjoyable little Indian summer, but when it became a real effort, and then a mockery, it made me sad: being forced to fake something which had been such an important pleasure was far more depressing than doing without it.

It seems to me that once one has got over the shock of realizing that a loss is a symptom of old age, the loss itself is easy to bear because you no longer want the thing that has gone. Music is the only thing I would really like to have back (whisky would be nice, but not nice enough to fret about). If a hearing-aid is developed which truly does restore their real nature to those nasty little scratchy sounds which make silence seem lovely, then I will welcome it.

The big event of old age – the thing which replaces love and creativity as a source of drama – is death. Probably the knowledge that it can't fail to come fairly soon is seriously frightening. I say 'probably' because to be as frightened as I suspect I might be would be so disagreeable that I have to dodge it – as everyone must, no doubt. There are many ways of dodging. The one I favour is being rational: saying 'Everyone who ever was, is and shall be, comes to the end of life. So does every *thing*. It is one of the absolute certainties, as *ordinary* as anything can be, so it can't be all that bad.' Having said that, you then allow your mind to occupy itself with other matters – you do not need to force it, it is only too pleased to do so.

And I have also been granted another specific against unseemly fear, which is remembering the death of my mother. She died in June, 1990, the day before her ninety-sixth birthday. That week she had bought a eucalyptus tree, and Sid Pooley, who with his wife had been working in her garden for years, came to plant it for her. She went out to show him where, and when he looked up from digging the hole he saw that she was not quite herself. 'Are you all right?' he asked, and she said she was feeling a bit odd and had better go back to the house. When Sid had helped her back and put her into her chair in the sitting room, he telephoned Eileen Barry, her home help and friend, who came quickly. Having had much experience of old people, Eileen suspected heart failure, so before telephoning me and my brother she got my mother into the little cottage hospital which we are lucky enough still to have. It used to be run by Anglican nuns who have a convent in the village, and my grandfather was one of its founders. At that time it had only two private rooms and two wards, one for old women, the other for old men (most of its patients are very old: younger people are treated at the county hospital. An elderly cousin of mine, on hearing a rumour that our little hospital might be closed, exclaimed: 'Oh no! Where shall we die?'). Both the rooms were occupied, and the women's ward was full, so they found my mother a bed in the men's ward and put screens round it.

I got there, after a misleadingly reassuring telephone call, early next morning, and found my brother Andrew and my cousin Joyce beside my mother's bed. My sister could not be there because she lived in Zimbabwe. It was frightening: my mother's face was almost purple, she was gasping for breath, and they told me she had just vomited black stuff. It seemed that she must die at any moment. When I put my hand on hers and leant over her, she opened her eyes, which wandered for a moment and then met mine – and a wonderful thing happened: a smile seemed to come flaming up from deep inside her, illuminating her whole face. Andrew was to say later 'That was an *amazing* smile she gave you,' and so it was: the complete expression of a lifetime's almost always unspoken but never doubted love, coming to me like a precious gift.

Eventually a doctor came and gave her a shot – morphine, I suppose – and one of the little rooms was made ready for her. She fell into a deep, drugged sleep and the sister in charge said firmly that nothing was going to happen that night (the day had seemed endless – it was astounding to realize that it was over), so we had better go away until next morning. Andrew drove off to his home sixty miles away in north Norfolk, and Joyce and I went to my mother's house, fed her dog, scrambled some eggs and went to bed – I in my mother's bed, which felt odd but comforting.

And next morning she was better, sitting up against a bank of pillows in her quiet little room, pale but like herself. Her voice seemed almost strong when she said 'Oh darling – could you brush my hair? It feels so horrible.' When I had done that I went to find Sister, exclaiming when I did so 'She's much better!' That kind woman put her hand on my arm and said: 'She's *feeling* much better, but she is still very very poorly' – and I understood that she was warning me not to expect recovery.

All that day my mother was sleepy, but herself. From time to time she murmured that she would like a sip of water, or the bedpan, and she told me that although her desk looked untidy I would find her will and other necessary papers in one of its drawers. 'But Aunt Kit,' said Joyce – my mother's eldest niece, and the one dearest to her – 'you'll be back there yourself in a few days,' to which she answered sharply 'Don't be absurd, I could go any minute.' Twice she emerged from a doze into a state of slight confusion, once thinking her dog had been in the room, then reminding me to pay for the wreath of poppies she put on my father's grave every November, which was five months away. The next time she woke, after quite a long sleep, she said: 'Did I tell you that Jack drove me over to Raveningham last week to buy that eucalyptus?'

'You told me he was going to,' I said. 'Was it fun?'

And she answered in a dreamy voice: 'It was absolutely divine.'

Then she turned her head away and went back to sleep.

Jack, who drove her that afternoon, told me later that it *had* been an exceptionally lovely day – June at its most beautiful – and that she had asked him to go by a lane she specially loved because she often rode that way as a girl. 'She did enjoy every minute of it,' he said.

A few minutes after she had fallen asleep Joyce and I decided that we had better go to feed her dog, and before we had been in her house fifteen minutes, Sister telephoned to tell me that she was dead.

The nurse who let me into her room when I went back to say goodbye to her was embarrassed because, although they had closed her eyes, they had not propped up her chin. She looked just as she sometimes looked when she went to sleep in her chair with her head leaning back, so that her jaw dropped: not a dignified deathbed image, but too familiar to be distressing. And anyway, I was far from distress. I was full of gratitude because she had come to the end of her days with an image in her mind of an afternoon that had

*My mother in her garden*

been 'absolutely divine'. One dreadful day, one of sleepiness, then that. She had bequeathed me, as well as that wonderful smile, the knowledge that an old person's death is not necessarily terrible.

That a woman of ninety-six was lucky enough to die an easy death without losing her wits or the ability to enjoy her chosen way of life in her own house: there was nothing much to mourn in that. Naturally I was to miss my mother – would often catch myself thinking that I must tell her something amusing or ask her something important – but I would also come to feel that mothers are never quite lost. Increasingly I see how much of her is still with me, literally in that I carry her genes within me, and also because of how much my attitudes and outlook were shaped by the upbringing she gave me. And when she died I avoided – though narrowly – what is sometimes the worst part of mourning: the burden of guilt about the dead person's last years which can threaten people after a parent's death.

My mother would never have dreamt of saying that she was

lonely and sometimes afraid, but of course she was; and it became worse when, a few years before her death, she began to have attacks of vertigo. She knew they were not dangerous (unless one of them caused her to fall dangerously), but they were very unpleasant and enduring them alone called for considerable courage. My brother and I bullied her into accepting one of those lockets which send out an alarm call, but we couldn't make her wear it. I knew she ought to have someone living with her – and I also knew how relieved and happy she would be if that someone was me.

Because I was one of the founding directors of the publishing house André Deutsch Limited, I was still working there, and I still needed to work. Publishing had been rewarding in many ways, but not financially (partly owing to my own indifference, which I now see as foolish, if not reprehensible). I had almost no savings, nor did my mother have any money to spare. She was the extravagant one in a set of sensibly frugal siblings, and although her extravagance was touchingly modest (buying a hundred daffodil bulbs instead of twenty, for example) it had left her in an awkward position. My father had retired from the Army as a lieutenant-colonel, so the pension paid to his widow was small, and although my maternal grandfather had set up a trust for his four daughters which no doubt seemed generous when he did it, by the time my mother reached her nineties it brought her in less than a thousand a year. Like her sisters, when widowed she gravitated home, which meant to the estate then owned by my uncle, where their mother still lived. My uncle sold her very cheaply a tumbledown cottage, and she somehow scraped together the money – helped, I think, by a sister – to convert it into a charming little house . . . and then found herself without enough money to live in it. Her brother came to the rescue. He bought back the now much more valuable cottage and let her go on living in it on condition that it would return to the estate after her death, so she was able to buy herself an annuity. It was a relief to her children that she could continue living in the house which suited her so well, but it did mean that if I were to give up my job she could offer me no security in return.

The truth was that I would not have much in the way of security whatever happened, so this was not really so much of a problem as I tried to think it was. I fear that I dwelt on it in the hope of convincing myself that I had a good reason for not moving in with her. It was hard to admit how appalled I was by the prospect of giving up my job – or more exactly, of giving up the life I had made for myself in London. My brother, who had a family to support, offered to have her to live with him if it became necessary, and it was not his fault that nothing would have made her accept life in someone else's household. My sister in Zimbabwe also had a family. I have no children, and the man with whom I live has always been as little possessive as I am myself, so theoretically I had the mobility to move in with her, and no doubt if we had absolutely had to we *could* have managed financially. But I, too, was an old woman, only twenty-one years younger than she was. I, too, had built myself a life which suited me, and the prospect of giving it up seemed to me dreadful. All the more so in that although I loved her, we had little in common beyond kinship, so when I was with her I always had to put my own nature on hold and exist in terms of hers. When younger, she had entered into her children's interests rather well, but by about her mid-eighties she stopped bothering to make the effort to do so. It was on her ground that we had to meet, and although I liked her ground, it was astonishingly exhausting to be cut off so completely from my own, even for the few days of a weekend. To bear it all the time, I felt, would be beyond me.

But during one of the many weekends I was now spending with her she had an exceptionally severe attack of vertigo. I was sitting up late over some work, so I heard the thump as she fell down in her bedroom. I rushed upstairs and was able to heave her into a chair, wrap a blanket round her (she went ice-cold during these attacks), and supply her with a basin before the retching began – the way the dizziness affected her like sea-sickness was the worst part of it. Usually the attacks lasted about half an hour, but this one went on and on. There was nothing for me to do but hold her head and add to her wrappings, and as the night went by I became frightened. Every now and then she gasped 'It will pass, it will pass,' but it didn't, and surely the strain of all that dreadful retching must be more than her poor old heart could stand? So I decided to call out the doctor. He came quickly, gave her an injection, and stayed with us to make sure that it would work, which it soon did. As I helped her into bed at about three in the morning, I realized that the time had come when I *must* take action.

I decided on a compromise: from then on I would divide each week between London and Norfolk, three days in the office, four with my mother. When I was not there I would gamble on her being kept safe by Eileen Barry early every morning, Sid and Ruby Pooley looking in every afternoon, and the generous alertness of kind neighbours (oh, the luck of Sid, in fact, being there when the time came).

Even that limited sacrifice of my own time seemed painful at first. The day I arranged it with the office and announced it to my mother, I collapsed with what I thought was flu, but understood two days later, with shame, to be nothing but strangled protest. It is extremely humbling to remember that my cousin Joyce, who like me was only twenty-one years younger than her mother and who adored her own house, moved in with my aunt full-time for months and months and never gave the slightest hint of boredom or regret. But once the first resistance was over, the arrangement worked well. My mother was happy – knowing there would be no more than three days alone seemed to make it feel less like loneliness and more like waiting for something agreeable to happen – and her happiness made me glad. And when she died, if I had believed in God I would have gone down on my knees and thanked him for the extra time I spent with her during her last two years.

What caused the kind of grief that twists the guts was not losing my mother, but losing the place where she lived which, wherever I myself happened to be living, had always been 'home'. My maternal grandparents' estate in Norfolk, just across the border from Suffolk, was where my mother, her siblings, her children and most of their cousins were rooted. This was because my grandmother was so much loved by her four daughters and her son that they all came back to her whenever they could, bringing their children with them and leaving them with her when they had to live abroad. Her son was a cavalry officer and her three married daughters chose military husbands, two in the Army, one who moved from the Army to the RAF after being one of the founder members of the Royal Flying Corps, so a good deal of living abroad went on. My brother and sister and I spent a large part of our early childhood and all our teenage years in the Hall Farm, just across the park from my grandparents' house – which we thought of as 'Gran's house' because my grandfather died when I was six. When it passed to my uncle and then from him to his daughter, the house ceased being the magnet it had been previously, but its land, the two little villages within its sphere of influence, the local market town – all that went on being 'home' while my mother lived there. Driving from London, when I reached the market town and turned into the road which I had traversed hundreds of times more often than any other road, I used to get – still get – an extraordinary feeling of entering my own body, as though I had become something like the giant human figure that was on display in the Dome and was at the same time a person moving through it.

It took us a month or so to sort out my mother's possessions and prepare her house for its return to the estate, which promptly sold it – luckily to great friends of ours. Then, one day, I suddenly realized that I was driving that road for the last time. I would of course be returning to Norfolk to stay with my brother, or with Joyce, but I would no longer have a reason to drive this way – and the thought of doing the trip not because I was coming home, but just to see what was going on there, seemed so horrible that I almost wept. Realizing it was ridiculous to mind so much, I made a great effort to reason myself out of this grief, but was successful only on the surface. It did not occur to me that the grief might soon be dispelled.

This happened thanks to my cousin Barbara, to whom I already owed my home in London. Although she is eight years younger than I am we have been friends since the mid-fifties when, soon after coming to London for her first job, she was looking for somewhere to live and I had half a flat to offer. It was very much a young person's first flat, with nothing on its floors but dingy underfelt, and a sparse collection of furniture cast off by other people; but it was large enough to take a lodger, which helped us to pay the rent. When Barbara, after finding her way into political journalism, married the lodger, I moved off to a happy spell in Chelsea, sharing a house with a friend; but some years later the ground shifted simultaneously under both Barbara's life and mine, she bought a large house and I moved into it with her, renting its top floor. And when eventually my ineptitude with money made me unable to afford even the modest rent I had been paying, Barbara let me go on living there anyway, so that I have continued to enjoy a life civilized far beyond my means. Without her generosity I and my old companion would, by now, be living in a pair of bedsitters in Stoke Newington . . . in other words, our gratitude is inexpressible.

Barbara's mother, like mine, had been drawn home after her husband's death and had bought and converted a cottage on the estate – just one field separated the sisters, who had tea with each other every day. My aunt was the older of the two, but she outlived my mother by eighteen months; and she, whose husband had retired as a general and whose scrupulous frugality ought to have been a lesson to us all, was able to leave her house to her son and daughter. They agreed that Barbara should buy her brother out, and Barbara then suggested that I should add a room to it (André Deutsch added enough to my savings to make this possible), thus making it just large enough for us to share it as a country retreat. So here I am, still driving that old road almost every weekend, which has made the difference between a bearable old age and a happy one, and has given birth to this book.

Something I like about old age is that you can so easily let your mind drift. The present no longer contains much that demands concentrated thought: no more love affairs, no more work excitements or problems, no more (or very little) planning of entertainment or travel. Day-to-day life is so much simpler and more repetitive than it used to be that you can allow your mind to wander. The best times for it are in the morning, snug in bed putting off getting up, and in the evening, idling one's way towards sleep. Sometimes I find myself telling a story which has grown out of some small incident – perhaps a man in the park that morning was humiliated by his lack of control over his dog, and a mini-drama weaves itself round him. Or I have heard that a friend is ill, and spend a long time recalling her and her ways, imagining her feelings, foreseeing her future. Often I choose a time or place and let myself loose in it: Venice on a September morning, perhaps, or Santa Fe full of flowering lilacs as it was when I once spent a week there. One scene will lead to another, one event connect mysteriously with another of a different kind, and people I haven't thought about for years will materialize. And since the place where I spent my childhood has been restored to me . . . well, everyone knows that what comes back to the old most often is their distant past, and that is confirmed again and again in my own experience. In the last two or three years I have learnt what a vast amount of my childhood is stuffed away below the level of consciousness, much of it probably never to emerge but a surprising amount of it ready to become available, and all of it *there*. It has become obvious that what an old person is – provided he or she has not gone gaga – is not just the deteriorating body going through its necessarily simplified and sometimes boring occupations, but a mobile reservoir of experience.

Being this reservoir expands one's sense of importance, but because people are usually unable to benefit from experience which is not their own, it is better not to talk about it too much. Perhaps it is otherwise in societies which traditionally revere their elders (lucky old them!), but not with us. Generally what one has to expect is that the accumulation so essential to oneself is destined to vanish quite soon in a puff of smoke out of a crematorium chimney. (In fact it won't have even that amount of visibility: how a modern crematorium deals with the smoke problem I do not know, but certainly it is not allowed to upset the neighbours.)

The knowledge that this is so must, I suppose, be one of the chief triggers of autobiography. 'But if I turn it into a book,' one feels, '*there it will still be.*' Whether anyone will want to read it is up to them: at least it will be there for whoever does. I have acted on this impulse twice before, once in relation to my experience of love (*Instead of a Letter*), once in relation to my life in publishing (*Stet*), and both times there was a fair number of people who wanted to read the resulting book; so now, when what has bubbled up asking for the same kind of expression is the material at the bottom of the reservoir – the stuff which, on the whole, causes a person to be what he or she is – I dare to do it again.

*Aged seven, with my brother Andrew and little sister Patience*

# THEN

# LESSONS

I LONG TO BE a fish, water flowing as easily through lungs as over skin and allowing supple movement or lazy suspension. I lean over the rail of the bridge which spans the weir, and stare into the pool below it. Brown yet transparent, with golden gleams, like clear dark jelly. It makes me lick my lips with thirst.

The summer of my ninth year was hot, so the lake was low and only a little water spilt over the weir into the pool. After heavy rain it roared over and to prevent a flood the gate in the weir's bowels was cranked open so that, in addition to the overspill, a flying buttress of water escaped lower down, out of the lake's depths. Today's trickle was less exciting, but it allowed the pool to lie at peace. It was hard to decide between violent beauties and tranquil ones because things ought to have an order – good, better, best – and when they didn't it made me uneasy. But if it was impossible to decide between the tumultuous weir and the still pool, at least it was obvious that each was best when it was 'most' – and the pool today could not have been more what a pool on a hot summer day ought to be.

There were yellow water-lilies – wild ones, which I believed to be rare. The ones up in the garden, big and white with golden centres, were specially planted and originated in the Orient (was I told that, or was it just that they looked like it?), and that was surely usually the truth about water-lilies. We might be the only people in England who had wild ones growing in their pools as though living in India or Persia . . . one of those places from which precious things came. And my uncle saw a kingfisher here. All I could see now were dragon-flies zigzagging swiftly between hover and hover, and a moorhen stepping through the grass near the bridge, probably a parent of the eggs my brother and I ate that spring. The nest was anchored beyond arm's reach, so we took the eggs with a spoon tied to a long cane. Luckily they were new-laid – cracking a moorhen's egg was always an anxious business.

The contents of an egg which was too far gone echoed other horrors: there was sometimes, for instance, a dead animal hidden in long grass. The gamekeeper's 'larders' in the woods – wire strung with the rotting corpses of weasels, stoats, rats, jays, carrion crows and other threats to his pheasants and partridges – these were bad enough, but I knew where they were and could avoid them, or if I had to pass one because I was with someone who might think me silly, I could steel myself in advance, and look away. But sliding into a ditch to get at a clump of primroses: then, if there was suddenly a dead animal, my very blood recoiled. The worst was last summer, wading through a field of wheat (though trying not to trample it down, which was forbidden) for the pleasure of being in all that gold and smelling its warmth. My foot came down on a dead rabbit. Swerving, I almost landed on another, and realized that all round among the wheatstalks, partly hidden by the undergrowth of weeds, were collapsed skeletons with their loathsome tatters of fur – a sort of rabbit graveyard: how to escape without treading on another? Then panic sent me plunging out of the wheat. I could remember it only in quickly blinked-away glimpses, it was so dreadful. It did not stop me walking again through tall growth, or climbing into ditches, or exploring woods, but I was much more careful which diminished the pleasure.

It was a puzzle, the way things were rarely exactly what they ought to be. If I had run myself into a sweat, and the grass was so soft and green that it should have been caressing when I flopped down in it, there was usually a thistle or a hidden stone, or after a few seconds my legs would start to itch because of ants crawling over them. And if music started to climb higher and higher, instead of going up into absolute height it always turned and came down again. Height, depth, softness, sweetness – there was never quite enough of them. 'Why can't all food be sweet?' I had asked not long ago, and the answer was 'You couldn't have sweet if you didn't have sour'. What a senseless rule!

It wasn't like that in the serial story I told Andrew every evening, when we were in bed. The story was called 'Hal's Adventures'. 'Why Hal?' my mother asked – we knew no one of that name – and I explained that it was short for 'Halbert'. 'But there's no such name. There's Albert or there's Henry – Hal is short for Henry.' I could not accept that because the abbreviation of Henry must so obviously be Hen; so Hal went on being short for Halbert, my hero who could command magic at a pinch and was absolute ruler of his people.

Hal's closest friend and lieutenant was Thomas, who was trusty and also dull: all I bothered to know about him was that he had brown hair (Hal's was auburn) and blue eyes. Thomas had a pretty princess with curly golden hair, but Hal's princess was dark and tragic-looking, with hair that fell to her knees in smooth waves. If I could have had my way the story would have consisted almost entirely of what the princesses were wearing, what kind of horses they were all riding, what jewels adorned their chariots and thrones, what silks were heaped on their beds. Everything in their palaces was what it should be – all the food as delicious as strawberries and peaches, all the colours luminous. Once Hal and his entourage discovered a river of perfect beauty. Its water was as clear as diamonds and it ran over a broad smooth bed of spring-green grass.

My brother wanted events, not descriptions. I was bad at these, although I knew that marvellous things must happen in Hal's world if only I could hit on them. Since I couldn't, it always ended by being another battle between Hal's forces and the Pubbies.

We had set out to invent a whole secret language, but it had stopped at a special grunt for 'goodnight', 'jolyon' for 'penis', 'jellybolees' for 'buttocks' and 'pubby'. I felt ashamed of our lack of seriousness when we gave up. A pubby person was a person we despised: fat, soft, silly, scared. The Pubbies in the story were an obscene and treacherous army, always defeated, and tortured when taken prisoner. Once Hal and Thomas made them sit naked astride a wall with jagged glass on top of it, and bounce up and down – a stroke of genius which went down so well with Andrew that it often had to be repeated.

The worst thing we ever did to a pubby in real life was to push him into a bed of nettles as though by accident. Usually we went no further than acting aloof and showing off. The pubby would be handed over by its parents and our own – 'Why don't you take Michael to see the calves?'– and after a greeting which adults would think no worse than shy, we would start running along the tops of walls, jumping up to catch a branch over which to somersault, throwing stones at things (risky, because to miss made you look silly). If after a while the pubby joined in and proved as able as we were, he would be promoted – often with enthusiasm – to friend. If he was nervous, or didn't like to get dirty, or was simply not interested, he was condemned.

I would never forget the day when I stood by myself on the bridge because it had so much in it: it was summer; it was in this place – our grandparents' home – which all of us children felt in our bones to be our own; and it was near water. And perhaps also because I was alone, although I wasn't really. Andrew and two of our cousins were quite near, climbing trees. I was separate because I was sulking. Their enthusiasm for tree-climbing had outweighed mine for something else, and 'She's sulking, she's sulking,' they had jeered. The way to lift sulks above absurdity was to enlarge and prolong them. If I didn't speak another word all morning – no, all day – that would show them. At first they wouldn't notice, then they'd be puzzled, then alarmed. By the evening everyone from our grandmother down to Patience, our little sister, would be pleading with me to speak, or tiptoeing about, consulting in whispers as to what should be done . . . But while we were running down the slope of the park to the edge of the lake, and making our way along it towards the weir and the bridge, I felt resolution failing: words and laughter were almost escaping. I stayed by the bridge to save what dignity I could. By the time I heard shrieks of 'A hornet – look, a hornet!' my immersion in the things I was watching had purged me of resentment so that I could run to see the hornet (there was a nest of them in one of the trees) without noticing that I had capitulated. I remembered it briefly that evening: a whole day – how it would have impressed them all! But what could I do about my own frailty?

Childhood is so often remembered as summery presumably because summer is the season allowing children in northern climates the most freedom: the longest holidays come then and they can be out of doors, away from the adult-organized house – most themselves. That water is so central is harder to explain. A classic Freudian interpretation is that water and sand represent urine and faeces, essential playthings because with them the child can act out infant fantasies . . . Can that be true? With us the fascination of water coincided through early childhood with an acknowledged interest in urine and faeces, so there was no need for the latter to appear under a disguise. When we were seven and five years old my brother (who was the younger) asked me: 'Which do you like best, bigs or littles?' I knew just what he meant: these things existed in our minds as a subject, in the same way that interior decoration might exist in the minds of adults. When he said 'I like bigs best' his preference left me incredulous, as though he'd said 'I like garden gnomes'. To me littles was far more attractive – when I fell in love with the gardener's 'boy' I imagined him urinating, and I went through a phase of doing it myself in odd places – under a corner of the carpet in the bedroom for example – leaving a few drops here and there like a dog establishing its territory. It did not occur to me that urine smelt: I was stunned when this habit was discovered, and so frightened and ashamed that I must have known all along that I was committing a bad breach of the rules, even though I hadn't thought about it. I was caught while staying in an aunt's house, and my flustered nanny shut me in my bedroom, where I waited for some unimaginable punishment contained in the thought 'They will tell Mummy and Daddy'. I had never been smacked, never deprived of anything I wanted, never even sent to bed or stood in a corner – well, yes, stood in a corner once, but it seemed silly rather than mortifying. Adult disapproval was the only weapon used against me, so it was fully potent: the unimaginable punishment might, perhaps, be that my parents' disgust would make them unable to love me.

My aunt came into the room. The only thing I was aware of was a longing to vanish. 'You *are* a disgusting little guttersnipe, aren't you?' said the aunt, disdainful rather than angry. When I understood that I need expect nothing worse than that, my relief was so great that I could hardly comprehend it. My parents would never know! (When I was home again a doctor came although I wasn't ill, and pronounced my bladder sound, but I didn't connect the two events.) The incident soon faded – but I never again experienced the impulse to pee in corners.

No, the disturbances caused in us by water were not the same as the titillations caused by urine. Water inspired sensations of longing or impulses towards creativity (many dams were built). Water running shallow over pebbles, humped to the shapes of the stones; or over sand, trilling in minute puckers of ripple; water still and shadowy over mud, disorderly and silvered where it broke against an obstacle; water in muscular swirls and eddies: each of its moods had its own quality and evoked its particular response. It frightened only when in flood, yellow with soil, carrying clumps of scum, moving too fast. There was a terrifying book on the nursery shelves about the Mississippi in flood and a family of children swept away, clinging to the roof of their house . . . A stream in spate, even the disciplined stream which bisected the kitchen garden, was suddenly related to the Mississippi and became a threat – but a fascinating threat. Water linked with poetry rather than with sex.

Dabbling in streams was not the only way in which we expressed the urge to make things. When it came over us it was always the same – a strong, almost tormenting need to do something – but what? Often it short-circuited into bad temper: 'What shall we

*Fishing for newts in the kitchen garden*

do? – Mummy, we don't know what to *do*.' – 'Why don't you go and dress-up?' – '*No!*' . . . everything anyone suggested seemed futile. But usually the urge had its own solution within it, needing only to be recognized. Was this the house-building itch? No. Was it the dam-building feeling? No, not quite. Was it the signal for going over to the farm and finishing the cave we were digging into the side of a straw-stack? No-o-o . . . not today. What about making a pig-mush? Of course, that was it!

Making a pig-mush had to be done by Andrew and me alone, because no one else had quite the right feeling for it. We had been given an enormous old iron saucepan, now chocolate-coloured with rust, which we left lying about in the bottom orchard (the one for cooking-apples and quinces) for months between each pig-mush fit, and sometimes had trouble finding. The pig-sty was near the orchard, and first we would go and look at the pigs because it was necessary to work up a feeling of love and pity. Poor things. *Poor* things, in that stinking yard where the muck came halfway up the fence (pigs were not kept scientifically in those days). Nothing to do but lie about in that muck all day waiting for their food, and when the food came it was always the same: meal made into a sloppy porridge with water. Never mind, pigs, you're going to have a treat now. We're going to make a pig-mush for you, we won't be long.

The basis of it, to give it body, was a few handfuls of the pigs' own meal mixed with water in the usual way. The mush's beauty lay in its other ingredients. Some were obvious, such as apples, carrots and wholesome-looking fresh green grass, but as the work progressed the creative fever would mount, and we would scurry about the garden and even up to the house, to beg from the cook. Six pink, six white, six red rose petals; a handful of mint; pinches of salt and pepper; some icing-sugar; two senna-pods (the taste would be disguised and they'd do the pigs a lot of good); a little duckweed? Why not. Then some crumbled Madeira cake and some asparagus tops, and two bruised peaches which had fallen off one of the trees espaliered on the kitchen-garden wall. We might even dare to pick a perfect one – a crime, but what an undreamt of delicacy for the pigs! It could take most of an afternoon before the saucepan was brimming and the feeling came over us that there wasn't much more to be done to it now. Then a thorough last stirring, and it was carried to the pig-sty and balanced on the fence above the trough. The pigs would come surging and squealing, and there was an anxious moment before the pan was tipped: it would be disaster if the mush splashed uselessly over a pig's thrusting shoulders instead of into the trough. An opening – quick! . . . and the mush would be poured. One panful between five or six pigs was gone in a flash, of course, but we were sure that quality made up for lack of quantity, and would stand gazing tenderly at the pigs, deeply satisfied at having gratified such an urgent need.

Once a year one of the pigs was slaughtered in the lower yard. It was a good thing to be a girl then, feeling no challenge in this. Andrew, at the age of six, was moved by a mixture of curiosity and bravado to feel that he must watch, but it never occurred to me to do anything but stay as far from the yard as possible. Our cousin John was unable to admit that he felt as I did, so the two little boys went down to the yard together. Johnnie gave way before it was through, which was lucky for my brother, who could bolster his pride by sneering. 'Johnnie was sick – he ran away and was sick into the beech-hedge – but I didn't mind it at all.' His face was still greenish as he spoke, and his eyes were furious and scared. I thought him a fool as well as disgusting.

And in spite of all that bravado over the pig-killing, it was I who had to kill the hedgehog.

Much of what we were taught by our elders we resented or at best endured; a great deal of it we were later to reject; but some things we accepted without question. These things went into our minds as the kind of lore to which additions can be made if experience warrants it, but which is essentially true. Into this category came anything to do with animals, whether tame or wild. This was accepted so readily because our elders' attitude towards animals resembled our own, and also because it was obvious that on this subject the grown-ups knew what they were talking about. One article of the lore concerned sick or maimed animals: they must be cured if possible, but if it wasn't they must be killed quickly and efficiently 'to put them out of their agony'. We had not only been told this, but had seen it in operation. Out with a gentle-hearted aunt, we had come across a rabbit in a trap. We had seen her tempted to believe that it was less badly hurt than it was, but conclude that it could only die a slow death; we had seen her find a heavy stick and, making an obvious effort to overcome pity and revulsion, kill it with a blow to the skull. Hindsight suggests that there was sometimes confusion as to whose agony was being ended, the victim's or the spectator's, but there was no sadism in it: we knew that a hated deed had been performed because it had the moral weight of a duty.

My brother and I found the dying hedgehog in the Cedar Walk – the ornamental plantation which girdled the kitchen garden. It could still move feebly, but something terrible had happened to it and there was a ragged wound in its side. Andrew stooped over it, and recoiled. 'It's got maggots.' I overcame my horror to peer. The hedgehog was rotting alive.

We knew we should kill it. We looked at each other, I hoping he would say 'I'll find a stick.' Instead Andrew backed away and said 'I can't.' This collapse put him in my hands. I could have tormented him with it, but instead I felt suddenly aware of my seniority, and protective. I didn't blame him for dropping his front – he was closer to me for it – and I knew that I must assume responsibility.

A hedgehog has a very small head and a body which, because of its spines, can't be gripped. I couldn't touch it, anyway – my revulsion was such that I could look at it only out of the corners of my eyes. Part of the duty is that death should be instantaneous, so it was out of the question to rain random blows on the hedgehog with a stick: I needed to find a weapon large and heavy enough to be sure of crushing its head even if my aim was not exact. We were near the boiler-house built against the outside of the kitchen-garden wall to heat the vinery on the wall's other side. 'We could put it in the stove,' said Andrew sickly. We knew that we couldn't, but it drew my attention to the building which had recently been repaired. There was a pile of bricks beside it. 'A brick,' I said. 'Suppose you don't hit hard enough?', and I imagined striking the blow only to see the hedgehog worse maimed than before but still alive. But if I put the brick on top of the hedgehog and jumped on it with all my weight . . .

Andrew backed further away. Telling myself, 'Don't think, just do, it's got to be done, don't think,' I ran for the brick, put it in place and jumped, all as fast as I could. There was a sensation rather than a sound of crunching, but I was hardly aware of it; it was as though I were running away from horror so fast that it couldn't catch up. But before I could in fact run I still had to kick the brick away to make sure the hedgehog was finished. I kicked it, and we bolted. Relief that it was over swept away the horror, and pride filled me at having been able to do the impossible. I felt strong, and Andrew was subdued by admiration, but there was no question of triumphing over him because we had shared the experience too closely. Soon we started laughing and pushing each other about. Many years later I was to hear someone arguing that the elation of soldiers coming out of battle after having killed proved the existence of mankind's murderous impulses. 'Fool!' I thought. 'The murderous impulses exist, no doubt, but *that*'s no proof of them. They're elated because they've *survived* killing.' I myself, although I didn't know it then, had used up my whole reservoir of courage for killing. Never again would I be able to put an animal 'out of its agony', however extreme that agony was.

In spite of this concern for animals ours was a hunting, shooting family: many pheasants, partridges, ducks and hares were killed every winter for its pleasure. No foxes – but only because it was not fox country; the hounds were harriers. The children and women often sprang traps set to catch the 'vermin' which might interfere with sport, but the women also walked out with the guns and most of them rode to hounds as soon as they were old enough to handle a pony. We were proud of the good shots and good horsemen among us, and aspired to a similar expertise. We and our cousins would have thought anyone arguing against blood sports thoroughly pubby.

I didn't want to shoot or watch shooting, though I didn't question that shooting was part of adult life; my brother was impatient for his first gun. He had no wish to hunt; I daydreamed about it from the day I was first taken out on a leading-rein. My preference for riding to hounds was determined partly by the fact that the rider does not himself inflict death and needn't even see it, and partly by the inexactness of my eye which meant that I would never be able to shoot well, whereas I was good at riding. Andrew had a good eye but lacked confidence on a horse. Both of us would have adored a tame fox or hare or pheasant, and liked stories of hunted game being saved from pursuers – we could imagine ourselves tricking hounds onto a false scent and sheltering a panting animal in our arms until it could run safely away. We had no inkling of the inconsistency of our attitudes.

The reason why enjoying blood sports and loving animals didn't seem contradictory to us was because the two things occupied different areas of experience. The sports were a matter of acquiring skills which were difficult and exciting to practise, of proving yourself able and brave, and of graduating to the status of adult. And not only did they seem as inevitable as the seasons, but they were felt to be particularly *ours*: class came into it, even for the very young. On the whole 'poor people' didn't hunt or shoot. Those who did, and were good at it, had special merit because their ability was surprising; those who did, and were bad at it, were comic. We felt that these activities and the rituals which surrounded them were somehow part of the superiority with which our families were blessed: an attitude so intrinsic to higher-class rural life at the time that you needed to be distanced from that life in some way in order to escape it.

Against this, loving animals was much like loving people: we didn't think of ourselves as 'loving dogs' or 'loving horses', but as loving Lola and Kim, Acoushla and Cinders. No one was personally acquainted with the animals which were pursued and killed – they were not unlike those distant Chinese children who, it was said, would be glad to eat up cold rice pudding. It was a pity that Chinese children were hungry, and it was a pity that game animals were frightened and killed, but what could you do about it? Whereas your dog and the pony you rode were your *close friends*, and what was more: they shared your pleasures. It was obvious that gun-dogs loved to play their part in a shoot, and that there was nothing a pony enjoyed more than being ridden to hounds.

Take Cinders, for example. He was not my first pony – that had been Molly, a dear old ambulant bean-bag whose role, played to perfection, had been to inspire trust. Cinders was my first pony for proper riding, with whom I continued until I outgrew him at about twelve; and he was a wicked bully. The theory was that because he had not been gelded until he was three, he still believed himself to be a stallion – and he did, indeed, chivvy the mares into groups and threaten approaching rivals although they were all twice his size. He also, when out to grass, used to bully children, so that trying to catch him was always a drama. He would flatten his ears, roll his eyes and chase us back over the fence, then swivel round and launch a kick in our direction as though mocking us. Often we would have to call our mother, who had mastered him

long ago by swearing at him in a loud voice and beating him with
a walking-stick. He never tried his tricks on her. It took me a long
time to summon up the same authority over him, but I finally
succeeded. And the lovable thing about Cinders was that once his
opponent managed to get a bridle on him he called it quits not
only with a good grace but with generosity: no pony displayed
more evident enjoyment in our rides, or was more eager to take on
a formidable obstacle when out hunting. Once we came to a place
where the way out of a field had been blocked by a sheep-pen –
a rectangle of hurdles – so that the jump was an in-and-out. I was
on the verge of hesitation, but Cinders would have none of that,
and bounced me over this double jump so stylishly that when, a
few days later, the Master of Hounds met my father he described
it as 'a splendid sight'. It must in fact have been nearer comic than
splendid – pure Thelwell – because Cinders was a tubby little
pony and I, at that time, wore round glasses and two short pigtails
which assorted oddly with the bowler hat *de rigueur* when out
hunting. But luckily for me, I was aware only of the glory of it.
Discovering that you were braver than you thought, and the

*On Cinders, when he was very young: 'pure Thelwell'*

delightful collaboration with your beloved mount: those were the joys of riding to hounds as far as I was concerned, and firmly though I turned against blood sports once I had grown up, I was never able to regret having once known those joys.

'You 'ont never do it *that* way, bor,' said our best friend, Wilfred, who was the cowman's son, when my brother was trying to knock a tin of paint off a beam in the loft by lashing at it with a piece of cord. He said 'bor' (boy) not because he was much older – he was the same age as I was – but because in Norfolk everyone was 'bor', just as everything was 'little' and 'old' ('That's a funny li'l old car', we might say, hoping to sound like our friend). 'You 'ont never do it that way, bor, that ain't the way to go about it.'

Piqued, my brother said snootily: 'Why do you always say *ain't*? The proper way to say it is *isn't*.'

'You're wrong there,' said Wilfred placidly. 'The proper way to say it is *is not*.'

And snubs to us, I thought, with surprise and pleasure. It was not Wilfred's scoring over my brother that pleased me, but his scoring over both of us, because for a moment I had identified with the jibe and had simultaneously been made to feel uncomfortable by it. For a flash, we had both belonged to a world superior to Wilfred's, which had felt wrong. His answer had demolished that superiority and had given him a dignity which I wanted him to possess. I was, after all, in love with him, though not so passionately as I was with the gardener's boy who was romantically distanced by being in his teens.

If blood sports were as inevitable as the seasons, class differences were as natural as weather; and thus, like the sports, embraced contradictions which we failed to perceive. *Of course* Wilfred was our best friend – we itched every day for the moment when we could scoot across the park to the farm and join him – and a friend not only congenial, but admirable. He went to bed later than we did, for one thing, and ate tinned salmon which we were not allowed, and knew more than we did about farming matters. He was also more sober and responsible than we were, so if he condemned something as silly we expected him to be right. And he was handsome: I often put him in peril in my daydreams so that I could rescue him and perhaps even kiss him before he recovered consciousness. Yet in spite of all this he never came into our house and we never went into his. We might call for him, or he for us, but then the caller would wait shyly by the door while an adult summoned the one called on. And neither side even noticed this.

In spite of taking class too much for granted to question it, we were not unaware of it. We knew it because this whole place belonged to us (to our grandparents, but we made no distinction). The house, the park, the lake, the farm and other farms as far as we ever had occasion to walk or ride: all ours. No other house known to us was so big or appeared on yellowing postcards sold in the village post office. We knew it because when our mother overheard us boasting to a visiting child that the house had twenty bedrooms, she told us afterwards that we must never talk like that: it was ill-bred to boast of what you had to anyone who had less. We knew it because when I had been impertinent to a housemaid I had been sharply scolded: 'You must *never* be rude to servants because, you see, they can't answer back' (they could, and did – but it was true that they couldn't punish me: I saw that, and granted justice to the dictum). We knew it, too, because we had heard grown-ups ask 'Is he not a gentleman?' or describe someone as 'not quite', and the tone of voice was rich in meaning. There was nothing wrong in being a gamekeeper or a ploughman, a butler or a cook, a saddler or a tailor, but these people existed on another plane; and if someone who belonged on that plane tried to behave as though he didn't, he became both deplorable and comic. There was likely to be a strong taint of pubbiness about such a person, and our natural appetite for victims made this idea acceptable. Indeed, we found this little-considered but pervasive sense of class sustaining: one can hardly fail to feel the better for being sure one is the best.

It was rare, however, for us to be offensive – perhaps the *ain't – is not* incident was the only one of its kind between us and Wilfred. We had few occasions for the open exercise of snobbery: most of the people we knew were of our own class or else of the rural

working class which was shaped by economics and custom to fit in
with ours. Other people were more likely to be seen at a distance
than known. There was, for instance, a girl who came out hunting
in a top hat and patent-leather boots – a sort of music-hall parody
of the clothes worn for hunting in the shires, which even in its
purest form would have been 'wrong' in our county, where the pack
was an unpretentious one. We were careful not to look at her too
pointedly – it was embarrassing that she didn't know that she was
a figure of fun – and were civil if we had to speak to her. But when
we were among ourselves she was laughed at and despised, and
none of us questioned our own attitude.

There was, however, a counter-weight to class snobbery which
was felt particularly by children: humility about abilities
evidently superior to their own, and about things outside their own
experience. A lot of Londoners were said to be very 'common' –
but they lived in London! Even when very young these people
could find their way about in complex, noisy streets, knew which
buses went where, went often to the cinema, ate fish and chips,
ice-cream and tinned peaches . . . However unthinkingly our own
class-superiority was accepted in theory, in practice it was possible
for some 'inferior' person's gifts or sophistication to be seen as
impressive and enviable. The smugness was formidable, but it was
not quite leak-proof.

Being country children, we were inclined to despise toys: doing
something with real objects was more satisfying than playing with
sham ones. Beloved White Rabbit, back almost in my babyhood,
was a person not a toy. Andrew's comforter was a ragged bit of
shawl called Shollah Baa; Patience's was a blanket called Blanket;
mine was White Rabbit. He didn't have much hair, sat up on his
hind legs, and held a carrot between his paws: and I wouldn't know
that I'd thought of him as a person if I didn't remember so clearly
what I felt when they took him away.

He had lost one eye and his carrot, his ears had twice come off
and been sewn on again by Nanny, he was no longer white. But
what decided them – my mother and Nanny – that he must go was

that he'd started to leak sawdust into my cot every night. They must have had a discussion about how he could be removed without distressing me too much, and my mother must have been delighted when she hit on a solution: she went back to the shop where she had bought him and found that they still had his twin. So one evening when I went to bed I found, to my horror, a stranger lying on my pillow.

I howled. And the more they kept saying 'But look – he's just the same' the worse it was. How could they not understand that someone looking like someone else didn't mean that he *was* that person? They had taken White Rabbit away, and what had they done to him? Where was he now? He was all alone, he was lost – it was dreadful to think what he must be feeling . . . and Mummy couldn't understand that this silly white stranger couldn't possibly make it better. Indeed White Rabbit was not a toy: he gave me my first experience of grief for another's pain, and my first awareness that grown-ups could be fallible.

Later, I had just two toys worth playing with, the first of which was my farm. The lead animals arrived in flocks at birthdays and Christmases, until they covered a good part of the drawing room floor when properly set out. There were buildings, tractors, wagons and people, too – and fencing, though never enough of that. 'What do you want for your farm this Christmas?' – 'More fencing.' – 'Are you sure, darling? Isn't it rather dull?' They didn't see that I needed to enclose more land because it was absurd to have cows, sheep, horses and pigs all in one field, as they never were in real life. What I envisaged was a *proper* farm, with a realistic number of enclosures, even some fields empty of animals because they were down to wheat or sugar-beet . . .

The Meccano set, too, reproduced real things: cranes which lifted loads, bridges which could be winched up to let ships through. Because I was lazy, and was believed to have little practical sense, everyone was surprised when I commandeered this set which belonged to Johnnie who was away at school. I was clever with it, working patiently on elaborate constructions, and (as I'd been with the farm) anxious to possess more parts so that I could

achieve greater verisimilitude. But this addiction was so
uncharacteristic that no one trusted it to last, and Meccano was
expensive – so 'my' set was reclaimed by its owner, and I accepted
that my interest in it had been no more than a whim . . . accepted,
but with regret. I had an inkling that unrecognized capabilities were
being written off. And I was right. Many years later, first
needlepoint, then dress-making, then gardening were to prove that
I am indeed much better at doing things with my hands than my
elders, followed by myself, had supposed.

Laziness: it was laziness that made one drift in the direction
towards which they pushed one. In spite of the energy children put
into their activities, it is inertia which most threatens their
development into rational beings ('Why can't you behave like a
rational being?' an early governess, much despised, used to say to
me – so often that the expression became a joke, meaning nothing
but this woman's silliness). Our greatest pleasures were those which
were most accessible. Like almost all children we thought jelly the
most delicious of foods, and jelly is the food which offers least
resistance. Do what is fun, don't do what is difficult: that was the
principle we followed. And the grown-ups, recognizing that this
principle is innate in everyone, believed that our upbringing should
combat it. They thought it would be hard on us to grow up
unaware that people often have to do things they don't immediately
want to do – not only to fit in with other people but also,
sometimes, to reach ends desired by themselves.

   So you must wash your hands before coming to the table; you
must shut – not bang – doors behind you; you must remember to
say 'please' and 'thank-you'; given chocolates, you must offer them
round before eating one yourself; you mustn't shove or grab or
shout; you must go to bed without fuss when the time comes:
'manners', though considered important in themselves, were also
insisted on as being character-forming. The rules, laid down clearly,
reached back to a time before we could remember, so that following
them wasn't painful. We would not have observed them if we had
not been made to, but we didn't resent them more than any other

tiresome but inevitable thing such as thistles in grass or pebbles on beaches. It seemed natural to me that I should be made to conform to certain patterns of social behaviour, just as it seemed natural that I had to sit down to lessons, like it or not (though I should not have believed it if someone had told me that I would end up deeply grateful for having been taught how to parse a sentence).

In theory grown-ups, particularly our mother, would have liked to go further in character-forming. She saw the social viability conferred by these mild disciplines as minimal, and would have liked us to become individuals of exceptional ability and virtue. What we would need for this was 'will-power'.

She had a decisive, even slightly high-handed manner and bright blue eyes, so she used to appear formidable when she spoke of will-power. We understood it to be something by which the old Adam could be controlled, the lazy could become energetic, the stupid clever. Together with 'self-control' it propped an austere ideal: a way of life in which you were indifferent to comfort, ate only for the energy food provides, never thought about yourself, and accomplished great achievements.

It was an attractive idea. When I was about eleven it seemed to me that I only had to get the knack of it and I would be able to move mountains – or at least an oak tree (I was riding through the park as I thought this). I decided then and there that every day I would do one thing I didn't want to do, limbering up gradually to mountain-moving strength. As I advanced in the discipline I would become able to do long division, then my painful progress through Latin would become swift and smooth, and then greater rewards would appear – power not only over myself (might I become able to levitate?) but over other people and things. The kind of achievement will-power would make possible blurred in my mind with the rewards of faith, which were also sometimes canvassed, though in church and scripture lessons rather than by my mother. To silence a thunderstorm, for instance, by saying 'Peace, be still', as Jesus had done: I had failed when I tried to do that because the muscles of my will were still too feeble: I would have to believe *much* more strongly if I was going to bring it off. Surely getting out of bed the minute I woke up in the morning, or saying 'no' to a peach at dessert would be a small daily price to pay for being able to do that?

Not, however, one single step in this programme did I take: by the next day my mind was occupied with other things. And this was also exactly what happened to my mother who, in spite of her positive manner, was as far as any child from putting her principles into practice. However authoritatively she spoke about will-power, her only conspicuous exercise of it was in getting what she wanted; and although I didn't consciously compare the image of my mother as austere and puritanical with that of my mother in action, or draw any recognized conclusion from these obviously contradictory images, both images were nevertheless there: it was an evident fact of life that stern resolutions were more often broken than kept.

Luckily this was also true about pocket money. Just as Mum would have liked to have had will-power, so she would have liked to have been sensible about money. If her own upbringing had equipped her badly for this there was all the more reason to see to it that her children's equipped them well. Her usual slapdash way of handing out pennies or sixpences whenever we wanted to buy sweets or an ice-cream would obviously lead us to suppose money appeared from the blue whenever we wanted: it would be unfair to us and likely to lead to tiresomeness, as she knew from her own experience. So: 'From today you are each going to get sixpence a week pocket money, and you'll have to think very carefully how you spend it because you won't get a penny more.' Each time she said this we felt alarmed. Her manner was so firm that we couldn't doubt the reality of the tedious responsibility with which we were now going to have to live. How depressing, simply *not being able* to buy a pennyworth of acid drops on a Thursday because of Tuesday's fudge: trotting across the park to make delicious choices in the little post-office-cum-village-shop was one of life's pleasures. But it would be weak and babyish not to accept the challenge, so we would take our first sixpences and soberly resolve to do our best.

The first sixpences of a pocket money drive were always the last. What with one thing and another she would forget about it.

Once she had an idea about our upbringing which was supposed to be liberating rather than disciplinary. She had met a high-minded and progressive couple, and she must at that time have been in a mood of defiance against her own background. No doubt she thought it odd, at first, that their children called them by their first names, and even odder that none of their doors was ever locked, so that a child could enter the bathroom while its father or mother was naked in the bath, but after the first surprise she took to these ideas, suddenly seeing that the time had come to prove herself a modern mother. She came home from that visit bright-eyed, though a little less decisive than usual: she didn't say we *must* call her and Dad by their Christian names, only that we could if we wanted to; and that because it was silly and unhealthy to be embarrassed by nakedness, she *wouldn't mind* if we happened to see her without clothes. Clearly she was half-hoping for these innovations rather than ordaining them. 'Good heavens!' was what we thought, staring at her with a mixture of admiration and embarrassment at her daring. We saw at once that she was doing the sort of thing we did ourselves, defying the established order in a fit of 'over-excitement'. It was generous of her, but it was also foolish. We did try out their Christian names once or twice, for the fun of it, but 'Mummy' and 'Daddy' meant what they meant, whereas the names were empty, so there was no point in going on with it. And as for seeing my mother and father naked – that was a most uncomfortable idea. Child to child, nakedness was nothing; child to adult, it was outside our experience and ought to stay there. So progressive informality went the way of pocket money. Lines of conduct or systems of any sort, apart from those hallowed by custom, were too much trouble to keep up. Our laziness, although it was often chided by the grown-ups, was sheltered by theirs.

My own lack of will-power worried me in only one way, which fortunately cropped up only when lessons included doing sums. At these I was so bad that I felt it must be blameworthy. The others understood 'fractions' and 'decimals' quite easily, so surely I too ought to be able to understand them – surely if I tried hard enough

I could? I never did, so that must mean that although I felt that I was trying hard enough, I wasn't. I was never bullied about it – indeed, much kindness and patience went into attempts to help me – but I still felt twinges of guilt from time to time. It wasn't until many years into adulthood that I learnt something that suggested the incapacity was not my fault.

Five counters of different colours lined up on a table; the three-year-old child, already so good at the alphabet, being taught to count: one, two, three, four, five. I get it right at once and Mummy is delighted: 'Look, she can count up to five already!' But by the time an audience has collected the counters have been shuffled, and this time I say 'Five, two, four, three, one'. 'No, darling . . .' but I insist 'Yes'. They try again and again, until suddenly someone understands that I had never been counting, I had been naming. The yellow counter at the end of the row is called 'five', and it is still called 'five' when it comes at the beginning. They have to give up or I would be in tears at their misunderstanding. It was many days before I grasped what they meant by 'counting', and I was to remain a namer, not a numberer, for the rest of my life: a trait as innate as colour blindness, for which I could justifiably feel regret, but not guilt.

Guilt never caused me any serious distress, but humiliation did: humiliation, even if caused by something trivial, hit directly on surface nerves and was the sharpest misery I knew. To look silly. As soon as I took it into my head that something made me look silly, it became impossible to bear.

'Oh, do stop grizzling. Look, if you're really cold get down and run – that'll warm you up in no time.' Seven years old, I was perched on the front seat of the dog-cart between Mum and Revel, the groom. It was a bitter afternoon in January and we were bouncing over the frozen tussocks of Longmeadow, having taken a bale of hay up to some ponies out to grass. Much of the family's time was spent in such occupations, pleasures disguised as jobs and pursued as earnestly as any job. Revel could have taken the hay out by himself, but the dog-cart existed, yellow and black, elegant on its high wheels in a wasp-like way, and there was a young mare who would look good in it if she could be broken to harness. Mum was working at this, making use of opportunities to drive her out over the fields, getting her accustomed to being between shafts before taking her out to meet traffic on the roads. We had a car, so it was not necessary to have a horse and cart. It was simply fun that could be taken seriously.

Fun in theory, at least. To me, that day, it was extremely disagreeable. I had on my gum-boots, my fleecy gloves, and a huge scarf over my coat, crossed over my chest and fastened in the small of my back with a safety-pin. I was also wearing two jerseys, a liberty-bodice and a woolly vest, and my black velour hat with its domed crown and saucer brim – a sure indication of exceptional coldness, because we hardly ever wore hats. I was so bundled up that movement was difficult, and within the bundling I was becoming colder and colder, fingers going white and numb within the thick gloves, feet in agony within the socks lining the boots. Naturally I had been pleased to go out for this drive, because I took it for granted that the dog-cart was 'fun'; but now that we had turned towards home so that the wind was in our faces, pinching our noses to blue and making our eyes stream, I started to whimper and complain.

'Get down and run,' said Mum impatiently, pulling the mare to a halt. 'No, I don't want to.' – 'Oh, for heaven's sake – go on, hop down quickly.' – 'No . . .' and the whimpering became a howl. Couldn't Mum see what I could see: the dog-cart rattling off over the field, while behind – falling ever further behind – stumbled an absurd little figure, its gum-boots tripping over frozen molehills, its arms sticking out because of the thickness of its wrappings, its silly hat like a black mushroom bobbing against the white background of hoarfrost? *Think how absurd that figure would look to Revel!* So what if running would make me warm – I would rather die of cold than become that figure in this admired man's eyes.

'*Why* won't you get down?' asked my exasperated mother. 'Because it would be so silly,' I sobbed. 'But it's much sillier to sit here snivelling and freezing.' Howl – howl – howl, because that was true, and Revel, who was keeping out of the scene, staring ahead in an abstracted way, must already have thought me very stupid. But now getting down seemed worse than ever, because the ridiculous figure would be sobbing, its nose would be running, it would be a disgraceful spectacle as well as a comic one – not only my mind, but every muscle in my body locked in refusal of this humiliation.

Another humiliation, even worse, came at about the same time from a sudden reversal of my role in a public place. My mother had taken Andrew and me up to London on one of our rare excursions to buy shoes or visit the dentist. These trips were exciting because moving staircases, the underground, buses, taxis, lifts, crowds – all the commonplaces of London life – were unfamiliar enough to be glamorous. Mum, more beautiful than ever in her best clothes, became extraordinarily impressive because of her assurance: her certainty as to which bus to take, her ability to swoop through the dazzle and glitter of a huge shop straight from the door to the department we needed. To us London was high life, and its highest points were reached in restaurants.

Because the object of these trips was usually Daniel Neal's, the children's clothing specialists, or a dentist or doctor in the Harley Street area, we would lunch in one of Oxford Street's big stores: Marshall & Snelgrove, Debenham & Freebody, or John Lewis. That a restaurant covered a vast floor space and contained a great many tables made it all the grander to us – Lyons' Corner House would have thrilled us. We would be hushed with pleasurable expectation as the lift carried us up, watching the lift-man's skilful manipulation of his machine with admiration. Sometimes he had to adjust the level before the doors would slide open smoothly – an inch or two up or down, so that we could step out gracefully onto the silencing carpet of the restaurant floor. Then a black-gowned lady would cast a general's eye over the confusing vista of tables, single one out and usher us towards it. All would be bustle and tinkle, but muted, and the tablecloths and cutlery, being unlike our own at home, must surely be more elegant.

We knew in advance what we would choose from the menu:

fried fish, in its crisply golden coat of breadcrumbs, and fruit salad. We never had fried food at home because it was considered unhealthy, and all the fruit we ate, whether cooked or not, was fresh, so the jewel colours, bland texture and syrupy sweetness of tinned fruit salad was to us unspeakably delicious. We were sure that restaurant food was food at its rarest and best.

My romanticism made me relish these occasions even more than Andrew did. He, although he enjoyed the food and the excitement, never wavered in his certainty that the country was best, whereas I could easily be seduced by notions of sophistication and the *mondaine*. So when at the end of one such lunch he wanted to pee and I didn't, I was pleased to be left alone at the table while Mum took him to the cloakroom. I pushed my chair a little way from the table, hooked an elbow over the back of it, and began to examine the lunching ladies, seeing their hats, furs, gloves and handbags as very smart.

Suddenly it occurred to me that now I was on my own at the table, anyone noticing me might think me *alone in London*. They might suppose that I had been doing my shopping all by myself, was in the restaurant and had ordered my meal all by myself, and was going to pay for it all by myself with money out of my own pocket. How deeply impressed they would be if they thought this! Some of the ladies might be whispering to each other even now, 'Look at that little girl over there, lunching all by herself in a restaurant and so *young*!' This idea enchanted me, and I began carefully to adjust my pose to one of greater nonchalance and assurance. I let one hand dangle over the back of the chair while with the other I 'toyed' with a fork; I tilted my head at what I was sure was a graceful angle, and willed my face into an expression of blasé hauteur. My eyebrows arched, my lips drooped; with perfect conviction I felt my face become that of one of the beautiful mannequins I had admired in Mum's copies of *Vogue*. (They were 'mannequins', not 'models' in those days: 'models' took clothes off, rather than showed them off, being the people who posed for artists.)

I was so deep in this role that I didn't notice Mum and Andrew weaving their way back towards me through the tables. The first I knew of their return was Mum's furious whisper: 'For God's sake sit up straight and stop gaping – everyone will think you're half-witted!' I was too stunned by the humiliation of it to cry.

Incidents – and there were many – in which something wished on us by my elders seemed an affront to my dignity, or in which my own image of myself betrayed me into absurdity, were the cause of the most acute mortification I experienced, but it cannot be said that they harmed me. They resulted in dignity's becoming less touchy and more discriminating, and behaviour better judged. Perhaps a more delicate understanding of my susceptibilities might have hindered more than it helped: the quickest way to learn to avoid or humour wasps is to be stung by one.

The restaurant of a big store was not in our eyes what it was in our mother's, nor was the flavour of its food on our tongues what it was on hers. We saw grandeur in size and quantity, deliciousness in sweetness and softness. We were easily moved to admire beauty, but had no idea of 'taste'.

Satin was beautiful because it was sleek; pink was beautiful because it was the colour of roses. So pink satin was very beautiful. So if you could have an enormous room decorated in pink with satin curtains and upholstery, it would be breathtaking, and it would be even better if all the furniture were made of gold and silver, because gold and silver were beautiful for their shininess.

It was the same with pictures. Brightness and richness were what moved us – and also the picture's subject. In an illustration to a story about children lost in a forest, the children must look like real children and the forest must be elaborately leafy and thorny and dark: we were bored and disappointed if the shapes were simplified and the colours flat. However clever the use of a few flat colours, however enticing those colours in themselves, they were not showing us what we wanted to see. And if an illustration which grown-ups saw as deplorably vulgar *did* show us what we wanted, and showed it with an ebullience of detail and colour, then we loved it.

Luckily no one bothered much about educating our taste. Every now and then someone who didn't know us very well would give us for Christmas an artily illustrated book and we would ignore it; and every now and then some grown-up would make it clear that he or she thought comics dreadfully ugly, and we would think 'Oh well, grown-ups!' On the whole we were allowed to go on seeing the redness of red and the blueness of blue, even if that red and blue together were boringly 'obvious', and experiencing the sadness of sad and the happiness of happy, even if the story which embodied them was painfully sentimental. And there was plenty of more grown-up reading about if we felt like turning to it, which of course we would do sooner or later.

My favourite picture when I was about eleven, more evocative in my eyes even than illustrations by Edmund Dulac or Arthur Rackham, both of whom I loved, was a particularly insipid drawing of a princess in a fairy story by A. A. Milne. This princess, whose anatomy was quite lost in the swirls of her floating hair and raiment (indeed from the disposition of the swirls she could not have *had* any anatomy), happened to have features which I coveted: a swan-like neck and clouds of black hair. And her dress, supposing any body could have been found ethereal enough to wear it, was wonderfully becoming. The artist had studied Beardsley, so that feeble though the drawing was, it contained echoes of a dreamy decadence. Time and again I would turn back to it, unable to see why my mother and my governess could see nothing in it. To me it was the essence of unattainable elegance – and it was witty, too: there was something about the way the jewelled slipper peeped out, the fingers tapered and the necklace was implied by playful dots which suggested wit. A real Beardsley might have alarmed me. From this bad drawing I was getting as much pleasure and stimulation as I would get from a real Beardsley when I was older, without any reference to the artist's skill, simply because this, I was sure, was how the princess in the story looked and dressed. And when I discovered Beardsley I did not appreciate him the less for having been seduced by his feeble imitator: instead I enjoyed him the more because he reminded me of my princess.

'Art' was the engraving of *Dignity and Impudence* above the nursery fireplace, and the three watercolours by my great-grandfather on the wall opposite the nursery windows, only one of which was interesting because it was a little bit like the view of the gamekeeper's cottage near the weir although, disappointingly, it was actually a picture of some unknown place in Yorkshire. Later 'art' stretched to include two pleasant silvery-blue East Anglian landscapes by Arnesbury Brown, bought by my grandfather and much more attractive than the other downstairs pictures, most of which were all but invisible behind brown varnish. But – oddly – 'art' did not include the five best pictures in the house.

These were portraits of people I knew, so I didn't think of them in terms of artistry. They would have been bad if the likeness had been at fault, but since in all of them it was excellent I saw the drawings of my aunts Peggy, Joyce and Doro and of my uncle Bill simply as *them*, as a photograph would have been; and would have seen the oil painting of my mother in the same way if she had not loathed it so much that I had to suppose that there was something wrong with it.

They were all by William Strang, a painter chosen by my grandfather because – I guess – Strang's portraits made him think of Holbein. One of the most precious books in Gramps's library was a huge volume, to be looked at only with the utmost carefulness, of Holbein portraits. Because the faces revealed when you turned back the tissues between the pages were often quite old and plain, they did not interest me, but I respected them because we all knew that they were greatly admired by Gramps. There must have been something special about the reproductions to make the book so precious – and indeed, when I think of the book now what I see with my mind's eye resembles the real thing so convincingly that they must have been exceptionally good.

William Strang drew beautifully and was a gravely honest observer: his portraits do have much of Holbein's entranced delicacy of line and calm closeness of attention: Gramps had chosen well.

My mother detested her portrait because it was such a good painting of a self-conscious seventeen-year-old resenting the ordeal

*My mother, by William Strang, 1912*

of sitting for it. She had not wanted to be 'done'; and when told that she must put up with it had thought that she would be asked to change into a becoming frock, but Mr Strang said no, her beastly old blue serge would do. Then, when he sent her out to pick a few of the wallflowers which were struggling against the frost – it was a bitter day – and she jammed them into a glass just anyhow, expecting him to arrange them attractively, he simply left them like that. And then he wanted her raised up a bit so he made her sit on two cushions, only to go ahead and *paint* the cushions instead of making it look as though the chair were the right height, *and* he painted her hands all red and hideous, which they were of course, but only because it was such a cold day. And on top of all that she couldn't think of a thing to say to the horrid man, so he obviously considered her a bore, and because he was so bored by her he hadn't bothered to make her look nice. Given her own way, she would have burnt that portrait.

Almost ninety years later her nephew Philip, who now owns it, lent it to Norwich museum for an exhibition of Norfolk portraits. When I reached the room devoted to the twentieth century, there was Kitty Carr, dominating it. What an eye-opener! Not till that moment had I been able to see through my mother's prejudice to the painting itself, and fully recognize its quality. It was easily the best painting in that gallery.

If art was a small and random collection of objects, music was an even smaller thing: scales and 'The Merry Peasant' thumped out laboriously under the tuition of Miss Doe, who visited once a week from our local market town, and was kind but not inspiring. Luckily this dispiriting introduction was counter-balanced by three Gilbert and Sullivan records and one of Paul Robeson singing 'Water Boy' and 'Swing Low, Sweet Chariot', all of which we loved and often played, which had been bought by an aunt and lived in a dark corner of the morning room with a small dusty gramophone. And another, even more thrilling glimpse of what music might be like was granted to Andrew and me when we were taken to Norwich to see our first (and for a long time only) movie: *Ben Hur*. Among the incidental music to it (played, I suppose, on a piano in front of the screen) was Schumann's 'Träumerei', by which we were ravished, and which someone unearthed when we got home in a pile of old sheet-music on the morning-room upright piano. I was able to pick out a little of the right hand, and did so over and over again to our delight; though I think we were enjoying the screened images it evoked more than the music itself. This little sprinkling of musical seed would have to lie dormant for a long time.

My parents bought their first wireless (as we called radios then) when I was eleven and we were living for two years in Hertfordshire. We were allowed to listen at tea-time when Henry Hall's dance band was playing, and soon became addicted to our favourite tunes, but we never imagined seeing the music-makers in the flesh or even buying records. We had no gramophone in that house, and I cannot remember anyone having a wireless in my grandmother's. Even in my late teens, when I was besotted by tunes I had danced to such as 'Smoke Gets in Your Eyes' and 'I've Got You Under My Skin', my only way of submerging myself in them between the times when I heard them at dances was by picking them out on the piano or singing them in the bath.

What you have never had you don't miss: we did not feel deprived of entertainment, and thought it natural that going to London to see *Peter Pan* should be a unique event. We got our kicks from what was at hand: reading, riding, picnics, swimming in the icy North Sea, dances, acting in our own plays, Bonfire Night, Christmas, Easter, Harvest Festival. Unlike most modern children we knew who Guy Fawkes was and why we burnt him on Bonfire Night (though I am glad to say we were taught that he was a baddie simply because he had tried to blow up parliament, not because he was a Catholic – slightly surprising in a household so prejudiced against Roman Catholicism). Of all the feasts, Christmas was of course the best . . . but no public entertainment has ever thrilled me more than my first Harvest Festival.

The excitement started the day before, when we went with cousins armed with walking-sticks and thick gloves to a neglected field (I suppose its clay soil was too heavy to be worth cultivating) where the tussocky grass was full of thistles and the surrounding hedges, dense with brambles, were almost tree-high. It was the best place for picking long sprays of bramble loaded with blackberries, some already ripe, some still red or green – and that was what the walking-sticks with their hooked handles and the thick gloves were for. With these sprays, next morning, a leather-gauntleted aunt was going to wreathe the font in the church – and we also had to find bunches of scarlet hips and haws with which she could punctuate her wreath.

Every autumn has one or two days which are perfect, and this was such a day: still, sunlit, the sky's blue very soft, almost silvery, because of the faintest possible hint of mist in the air. A long vista on such a day resembles a Chinese scroll-painting, the lower parts of trees and hills delicately veiled, their tops clear against the sky; and even a close-up of a hedge is simultaneously softened and enriched by the atmosphere. And there is the smell of autumn, as faint and pervasive as the mist – leaves beginning to decay? The smoke of bonfires? Stillness, light, colour, scent – all combine into a perfection made poignant because soon – so soon! – it will be over.

The sweet sorrow of parting, sadness as luxury – it is odd that young children should be susceptible to such a feeling, but Andrew and I certainly were. We loved having tears brought to our eyes by the cuckoo's call, which seemed to us in certain moods like the voice of innumerable vanished summers; and the evanescence of autumn's perfection made our hearts ache in the same delicious way.

And the next day after this lovely one was going to be even better, because we were going to be allowed to stay up for the Harvest Festival service. Our usual bedtime was six-thirty (we were six and four years old, put to bed at the same time for Nanny's convenience). The service began just when we were normally being tucked in, but we would be there! We were going to be out in the darkness of night, under the huge red harvest moon, and then in the brilliant church, and then, when we got home, we were going to have not ordinary bedtime milk and biscuits, but *real supper*!

And the church truly *was* brilliant. As soon as we were through the door, there was the font under its rich wild wreath, surrounded by pyramids of fruit and vegetables with a vast and glorious golden pumpkin as the centre-piece. All the ends of the pews, the whole way up the aisle, had sheaves of wheat and oats and barley tied to them. The screen and the pulpit were lavishly decorated with dahlias, michaelmas daisies and chrysanthemums mixed with more wheat, oats and barley, and in each window's wide recess a different still-life had been composed, some of them including loaves of bread and baskets of eggs (custom dictated who decorated which window, and they vied with each other to splendid effect). It would have been gorgeous enough in daylight, and in the glow of lamp and candlelight it was magical. *And* – for us this was an enchanting finishing touch – there were bats flittering about up near the roof; *and* the hymns were the best we had ever heard. We were so much taken with one of them that we went on chanting it for days afterwards:

> We plough the fields and sca-a-tter
> The good seed on the land
> But it is fed and wa-a-tered
> By God's almighty hand . . .

I still sometimes sing that hymn when I'm driving, safely out of the hearing of anyone with a good ear.

Lessons, though accepted with docility, were not interesting and were always much the same whoever was being our governess because our parents subscribed to a system of home education called P.N.E.U. It supplied the textbooks and even, I think, the timetables, and it set us exams from time to time which it marked – not that anyone, parents, governesses or pupils, ever paid any attention to this ritual. The best thing about P.N.E.U. was that it disapproved of tiring minds, which meant that all the lessons were very short. Perhaps we sometimes did lessons in the afternoon, but if so it was not often: I can't remember any, and the importance of being out of doors was an article of faith with the whole family, so that the grown-ups would have been against it.

The first two of the seven governesses we had came into the category 'Nursery Governess' which meant that they taught Andrew as well as me. When he was sent off to his preparatory school at the age of eight, my schoolroom companions were my cousin Pen, and various daughters of neighbours who shared the cost of the governess with my parents. The nursery governesses were unlucky, because they superseded Nanny, whom we loved – and the first of them was the unluckiest because she was French as well. Her accent, her clothes, the way she used knives and forks, her nervousness of animals, her smell of eau de Cologne and her unhappiness all made her unacceptable. She suffered severely from the cold, hated the food, and must have felt miserably lonely, stuck away so deep in this foreign country in a household where the adults found her presence a bore and were no more than civil to her, and her charges were resentful. This forlornness was a guarantee of failure because, like animals, we responded to assurance in our handlers: lack of it made us uneasy and hostile, quick to take advantage of feeble gestures of propitiation and rebellious against inept attempts to be firm. What we learnt from her was two words of French – *tais-toi* – and the simultaneously exciting and shocking fact, hitherto unsuspected, that children can be cruel to adults.

The first of the real governesses frightened us and the single term that she was with us has become a little capsule of oblivion: I no longer have any idea of what she did or how our mother realized that she must get rid of her at once, only a vague memory of the relief I felt when she had gone. Surely if she had done anything dramatically cruel to us it would have stuck in my mind, so I suspect it was nothing worse than irritability and lack of kindness – which, considering that no one had ever been even the least bit nasty to us, would have been enough to dismay us.

After her came the regular governesses. They left quickly, if they were boring because we saw them off, if they were charming because they got married, until we came to dear Ursula who was absorbed into the family and remained with us until I was sent to boarding school at the age of fourteen. She ought to have been a failure because she was plain, but it took her only a few days to win me over, and my mother too. She was kind, sensible, funny, easy-going. She loved animals and she found the P.N.E.U. syllabus as boring as I did, so she varied it with agreeable inventions of her own. Everybody liked having Ursula in the house, and I was to feel deeply indignant on her behalf when I got to school and the headmistress described me as the least well-grounded girl who had ever come her way.

One of Ursula's strengths was that she fully understood the importance of horses: she was almost as good as Mum at mastering Cinders. She was the daughter of a country parson, and I suppose her family background must have been similar to our own.

By the time she arrived I had long stopped *being* a horse – grazing on green patches of carpet, drinking from blue ones, stamping and pawing the ground, shying when alarmed. That had ended not long after the wedding at which I, a five-year-old bridesmaid, had become a family joke by standing in the aisle whisking my fringed sash behind me and nibbling my posy of flowers. By age ten or so I had reached the stage of daydreaming the perfect horse, an exquisite grey, half Arab for the fine head and fiery eye, half Irish hunter for its ability to soar over huge obstacles. I would settle down to this dream with relish, first establishing the horse's appearance, then grooming it and harnessing it faultlessly, and the dream would trail off into frustration because the relationship didn't offer enough complexity. It felt much the same as those I would have a little later about dressing for a dance where I would meet someone to fall in love with, but it didn't provide enough material for the feelings to feed on.

Our real horses – or rather ponies – were not dreamt about any more than members of the family. There was never a time when I longed for a real pony, because I always had one. To begin with, one was put into a little wicker chair-saddle, sitting sideways on a donkey or the ancient pony who – wearing leather boots strapped over her hooves – pulled the lawnmower. Then, when legs had become long enough to straddle though not yet long enough to reach stirrups, there would be a soft felt saddle on dear old Molly. We never went on walks along roads anyway, and it was easier for a mother, grandmother or nanny to lead an animal across fields than it was to push a pram. 'Sit up straight', 'keep your heels down', 'don't jab at her mouth', were instructions given not in the form of 'riding lessons' but in the same way as 'don't talk with your mouth full' or 'shut the door after you'. By the time a child was enough in control to be let off the leading-rein she would be at home on a pony, and by the age of about ten she needed no encouragement to become enthusiastic about horse management.

For some six to eight years the books Pen and I most wanted to receive at Christmas and birthdays were horse books. I accumulated a big collection of them: not only stories about girls (it was always girls) and their ponies, but also technical books on horse care and training. After Andrew had gone to school, Pen and I spent hours in the harness-room cleaning bits, soaping saddles and rubbing neat's-foot oil into reins and stirrup-leathers to keep them supple. At twelve we knew all there is to know about looking after and schooling a pony, and could put our knowledge into practice. The only reason why we were good riders rather than excellent ones, and our ponies adequately schooled rather than faultlessly so, was laziness. Schooling a horse to perfection requires almost as much dedication and self-discipline as training to be a ballet dancer – tedious exercises must be carried out every day and never skimped – and we would go about it only spasmodically because the temptation of riding simply for fun was too strong. Therefore, although I could go well out hunting, I was not exceptional when the finer points of horsemanship were called for. In the show-ring, if I did well in a jumping competition I always knew it was the result of luck: my pony had *happened* to take off the right distance before each fence, whereas the serious horseman is able to contrive that it will do so. I felt guilty about this.

But not guilty enough to spoil pleasure. The extension of power offered by a pony, the ease and speed of movement, the tapping of unsuspected courage, the satisfaction of collaboration with another creature and of controlling it in order to improve that collaboration, the joy of fussing over it – of loving it – these, from the age of about eight to about sixteen were the most completely realized delights of my life. The smell of a pony was good to me. I would kiss its velvety muzzle with sensuous pleasure, and every shape and texture it offered was familiar and congenial to my hands. There was hardly a movement a horse could make which I could not interpret. A horse will rest a back hoof just to rest it, or again, in a slightly different way, because it needs to urinate. It is uncomfortable for it to urinate if the full weight of its rider is resting on the hollow of its back: the rider should pitch his weight forward onto its withers to allow it the necessary freedom. To see another rider failing to interpret this signal would anger me: how could anyone who rode be so insensitive and inconsiderate? And how could anyone fail to know that his horse was thirsty, or was about to roll, or was being chafed by its girth? The ignorance and stupidity – the *pubbiness* – of anyone who didn't understand horses was beyond question.

Each animal being different, it was naturally impossible for my relationships with all of them to be equally harmonious. With one it was straightforward friendship, with another a concerned and slightly anxious love because it was too highly strung for its own good. And with Cinders, of course, it was a mock-battle of wills. Even when he was very old, almost as broad as he was long, his blue-roan coat gone frosty grey, he was up to his tricks. I would go out to pass the time of day with him as he dozed under a tree, and he would make a lunge at me; I would slap his nose, laughing, and he would lower his head to present his little furry ears for a rub, apparently knowing it was all a joke as well as I did.

We all anthropomorphized our animals to some extent, but were usually prevented by the attentiveness of our observation from doing it to the point of sentimentality. Indeed, it might be more accurate to say that we came nearer to seeing humans as animals. The study of animal behaviour was not generally recognized as a science at the time – certainly the public was still unaware of its bearing on the study of human behaviour – but when popular books began to be published on its findings I felt that it was all very familiar: it was no news to me that the habits of a vole, a goose or a chimpanzee could be linked with my own.

*Me on Acoushla; Patience on Patsy; Pen on Zingaro; Anne on Nora, 1928*

# THE HOUSE

THE HOUSE AND estate which conditioned our lives and bred our smugness was not, in fact, what we and our cousins felt it to be: a place that had belonged to us 'for ever'. It had been bought by our great-grandfather, a Yorkshire doctor who had married money, and then was left even more by a grateful patient, a Miss Greenwood. The legacy must have been quite substantial because my grandfather, his only son, was given her name: William Greenwood Carr. And the 'county' pleasures of hunting and shooting were not, as they seemed to be, bred into our bones. That same great-grandfather's parents, whose generation had moved from the yeomanry to the professions (medicine and law), were serious-minded Yorkshire people who believed that the most valuable thing money could buy was education, and had sent their son to Oxford. There, being a lover of horses, he took to riding to hounds. His mother, unpacking for him when he came home at the end of a winter term, found top boots and a pink coat, and was deeply shocked. The young man was told that he had not been sent south to scamper across the countryside with a lot of idle spendthrifts – and was told it so severely that he never rode again, but channelled his love of horses into breeding handsome pairs of them to draw his carriage. Nor did his son, our grandfather, ride, except to jog about his farms. It was our parent's generation – some of them – who had taken to 'county' ways.

My grandfather in his turn would dismay his father while at

*Gran's house, 1920s*

Oxford, on his part of their climb away from their roots: an incident preserved not by family legend, like the top boots and pink coat, but in four letters in the mass of correspondence kept by my grandmother: four letters which happened to be among those that I read after her death.

They were written in Yorkshire in the late 1870s – my great-grandparents had not yet moved south – and were addressed to their son William at University College. The first was only a few lines – a shot across the bows that must have given Willy a nasty turn – announcing that Papa is so dismayed that he cannot at the moment say anything more: he will be writing at length as soon as he has been able to regain his composure. The second letter explains his shock. Willy had written to say that he had asked for the hand in marriage of Margaret Bright, one of the four daughters of the Master of his college.

On first reading I assumed from the opening lines of this letter that Doctor Carr was outraged because he supposed his son to have fallen for a girl below his station – 'What a pompous old horror,' I thought. The tone was too agitated to be just a matter of 'Don't be absurd, boy, you are much too young to think of marrying', which would not have been unreasonable. But I soon saw that I was wrong. Papa was in a panic, and the panic was at the boy's presumption: he was aghast at what Dr Bright – 'that distinguished scholar and gentleman' – must be thinking of the impertinent advantage taken of his hospitality by the boy he had so graciously invited into his house. It had clearly not occurred to Papa that Dr Bright, a widower with four daughters, perhaps made a point of inviting carefully vetted young men to tea as an obvious way to getting his girls married. Instead, Doctor Carr had suddenly and disconcertingly seen his own handsome, intelligent and soon to be well-off son in a new light: as a cheeky clodhopper from the sticks.

The intensity of his panic is made clear by a letter to Willy from his mama, written on the same day, and beginning 'Oh Willy, Willy, how can you have done this to me': 'this' meaning 'send Papa into such a dreadful state' rather than 'get engaged'. Her letter is one of mind-boggling self-centredness. She is apparently indifferent to the rights or wrongs of Willy's love affair, and concentrates entirely on what she is having to suffer from Papa's frantic reaction. She has taken to her bed; she is unable to eat the least morsel of food; her headache is blinding. There is a distinct suggestion of an habitual connivance between mother and son against the father, and what the mother seems to be attempting is a revival of this connivance, regardless of what has caused the trouble.

The fourth letter is also from her, written about a month later. In the interval Dr Bright must have let them know that he is happy about the match, and proposed bringing Margaret to Yorkshire to meet them; and Willy has written to Mama, asking her to be kind to Margaret, who will naturally be feeling nervous. Mama's answer begins: 'Dearest Willy, you ask me to be kind to Margaret because she will be feeling nervous. She cannot be nearly so nervous as I will be . . .'; and goes on for two sides about the suffering that she is bound to undergo.

Her letters persuaded me that there must be a gene for querulous self-absorption. One of her granddaughters was always puzzlingly unlike her siblings in being weepy and self-absorbed. It was a joke in our part of the family that you could safely bet on her bringing any subject whatever round to herself within half a minute. 'You've bought a pair of leather gloves? Oh, how I wish I'd bought leather ones instead of those silly woolly things I got last month . . .' As soon as I had read my great-grandmother's first letter I said to my mother: 'Good God – this is Aunt D.'

Possibly the plaintive Mrs Carr saw her husband's agitation as something inflicted on her, rather than as something to share, chiefly because she did not share it. Coming, as she did, from a family richer and higher on the social scale than his, she was unlikely to see the Master's daughter as beyond her son's reach. It was she who caused them to move south for her health's sake, and they would not have been able to buy such a fine house and so much land without her money, so for all her apparent feebleness she carried weight.

The Carrs made the move to Norfolk before my mother was born to Willy and Margaret, but it was not until she was five that the house was inherited by her father, who enlarged it. It was a substantial rectangular house built in the 1730s, overlooking a beautifully landscaped park and lake. My grandfather extended it into a U-shape and added a graceful terrace from which to enjoy the view. He reactivated a nearby kiln which had provided the bricks for the original building, so the new bricks matched perfectly; and because his taste ran to eighteenth-century reading and artefacts, so did the architectural style of his extension. Other newly rich men in East Anglia created mediaeval extravaganzas, but in him there was still much Yorkshire puritanism and common sense, which combined with my grandmother's academic background to give the family sobriety.

Having read history at Oxford, my grandfather had then turned to law, but he practised as a barrister for only a very short time before coming into his father's money, which must have been astutely invested – largely, according to my mother, in railways. She told me that he carried on his watch chain a little key, which meant that when the family travelled up to Yorkshire to visit relations they could have the train stopped wherever they wanted. She thought, too, that there was Carr money 'in that railway across Canada to the Pacific'. My grandfather was a good and businesslike farmer, and for years I assumed that the land was what the family lived on: but there must have been a considerable amount of money in the background, profitably invested, to allow him to enlarge the house so handsomely.

He also enlarged the estate, buying a wood here, a farm there, and when my mother was a little girl she and the sister next to her in age used to be given the job of taking the estate map down from the wall and colouring the new additions pink, 'like the British Empire'. This was gratifying, but was also seen as a bit of a joke. No fuss was made about it, but in my grandfather's house it was always in the air that being well-off was no excuse for getting too big for your boots: unseemly or irresponsible behaviour would be condemned as vulgar or (perhaps the family's most chastening word) silly. I think my grandmother's love for her William lent a pleasing glow to his background: it was from her I gained the impression that 'Yorkshireness' meant sturdiness and honesty. She was proud of the trace of Yorkshire in her husband's pronunciation of certain words, such as 'cassle' for 'castle' and 'larndry' for 'laundry', and her favourite Charlotte Brontë novel was *Shirley*, partly because Shirley was such a spirited young woman, but also because it gave such a good picture of Yorkshire's industrial development. Her affection for the aspect of the family which was furthest from being 'county' probably served as a useful pinch of seasoning in the spell cast over her grandchildren by her house and its surroundings.

Everything important in my life seemed to be a property of that place: the house and the gardens, the fields, woods and waters belonging to it. Beauty belonged to it, and the underlying fierceness which must be accepted with beauty; animals belonged to it, and so did books and all my other pleasures; safety belonged to it, and so did my knowledge of good and evil and my wobbly preference for good. Of course my mother was really more important, but hers was

an importance so vital that it belonged inside me, like the essential
but unconsidered importance of breathing; and at a pinch the place
could stand in even for her, and had once done so.

When I was about a year old my father, then an army officer,
was seconded to a frontier commission which was attempting to
confirm the boundary between Abyssinia (as Ethiopia then was)
and Eritrea. My mother could join him there if she wished to, and
to miss such an adventure would clearly have been absurd,
particularly since the most baby-loving of my aunts, still
unmarried, was living in her parents' house and would dearly love
to take charge of me there for the three or four months my mother
would be away.

I cannot remember those months, but I recognize two traces of
them. The first is that although the aunt was in some ways an
annoying woman, I would always love her with a special warmth;
and the second is that until I was about seven I used to have
irrational fits of panic: *Mummy has gone away and isn't going to
come back.* This would happen if she left me in the car and went
into a shop to pick something up, or if I woke up soon after going
to bed and the house was silent. I think that something inside me
was always capable of saying 'Don't be ridiculous, people don't
disappear without warning', but that did not prevent a violently
physical certainty of abandonment. In the car (these must have
been the panic's earliest manifestations) I would be crying by the
time my mother returned – and oh, the magic in her crossness at
this silly fuss I was making at being left for three minutes! In the
silent house I would make more determined efforts to reason with
myself, but still it would end in my having to get out of bed, creep
to the top of the stairs, and listen. Soon a door would open or shut,
and I would hear footsteps or a voice . . . Life downstairs was
going on as usual, after all, and I could return to bed in an ecstasy
of relief.

And now I think that possibly the way in which places,
particularly that one, would always matter to me – at some level,
more than people – was a third trace left by those months.

★

We did not live in our grandmother's house all the time, nor did the families of our two sets of cousins on our mother's side: our homes were where our fathers happened to be serving. But we were always there for holidays and always stayed there when our parents were unable to take us with them to foreign parts; and Andrew, Patience and I were there far more than any of the others. Our father retired from the Royal Artillery in the late 1920s – reluctantly, because he would have been posted to India if he had not done so, but my mother had refused to go there with him – and got a job in a company that mined mica which meant that he was either working in London or travelling abroad. From then on, except for a couple of years when we had a house in Hertfordshire, we lived at the Hall Farm on the estate and saw my father only at weekends. Hardly a day passed when we were not in and out of the big house.

Before that, for one whole perfect summer, I lived there without the rest of my family.

As a child, I was somewhat given to sore throats, swollen glands, and stomach upsets which were diagnosed as colitis – never enough seriously to interfere with my pleasures for any length of time, but

*The Hall Farm*

enough to make visits to doctors less rare than they were for others. This time the doctor was a bald one, with very soft hands and half-moon glasses. Like other doctors I had been taken to in London he lived in a dark and magnificent house which conferred importance on me and Mum when we entered it, and like all doctors anywhere, in my experience, he was kind and courteous and tried to amuse me with jokes which, although they were not funny, were pleasing: that such a dignified man should take this trouble was flattering. So was having a young woman in a white coat to help me undress, and the gravity of the ritual was impressive. I never thought of being anything but docile on such occasions, even when I had to swallow a barium meal: it was as though I had been given a part in a play, with Mum (my manager) in the wings to encourage me. It was important that I should not let us down.

After this examination the white-coated lady took me back to the waiting-room and gave me a solitaire board to play with, while the doctor talked to Mum. I sensed that my part must have been a bigger one than usual, and indeed Mum's face when she came to collect me was serious. 'Did he say what I've got?' I asked: and she replied: 'Yes, darling. He thinks you must stop lessons for a time. It's not anything to worry about, really – you haven't actually *got* consumption, but you see some people have a tendency to consumption – that means it's sort of asleep in your glands and if you were very run down or anything it might start up, so he thinks you ought to have a very long rest.' – 'Long? How long?' – 'A few months, I think.' – *'In bed?'* – 'Oh, no, darling, I don't think that's necessary. I expect you'll go to stay with Gran.'

In stories girls who had consumption died. They became frailer and frailer and more and more interesting – by the time Beth died in *Good Wives* she had become so weak that she said her sewing-needle was heavy, which had impressed me as much as it had astonished me. It was alarming to think of myself as one of this sisterhood, and I was subdued as I got into the taxi. Could I really have something that might make me die? I had not taken in the bit about 'asleep in my glands', only the word 'consumption'. For some minutes it was as though I were preparing myself to be very frightened, but before I reached that stage the impossibility of it had asserted itself – and besides, hadn't Mum said no lessons, and that I'd go to Gran's . . . Was I really going to spend a whole summer there, with no lessons: my idea of perfect bliss?

The taxi took us to Mum's club, where we were staying, to meet Dad for tea. He was waiting in the library, where several ladies were already grouped round little tables. 'Hullo,' he said, as we came through the door, 'What's the news?' – and I, fear dismissed, was suddenly aware of the drama of my situation. In a loud and boastful voice I announced: 'I've got consumption.'

'Sshh!' said my mother, blushing scarlet. 'You must *never* say that. Go upstairs at once and take off your hat and coat.' I was so dismayed that I was unable to notice how the ladies in the room had reacted, but I feared from my parents' expressions that they had been disgusted rather than awestruck. If consumption was no more to be talked about than constipation there seemed little point in having it, and from that moment I stopped thinking about it.

So did everyone else. Because the doctor had advised it, I was sent to Gran's, the windows of my bedroom were nailed open – a symbolic precaution considering that she allowed no shut bedroom windows in her house anyway – and I was given a goat to milk and look after myself, which was unmixed pleasure. Cows' milk, in those days, was not pasteurized, so did hold a real risk of tuberculosis. In fact TB was still a serious threat: not so long before, all the daughters of a nearby big house had died of it. But in this case it must soon have become apparent to everyone that the specialist's diagnosis was fantasy. My health that summer was excellent and the special attention soon faded away. My three favourite cousins, Joyce, Anne (the redhead) and Pen (the one nearest me in age) were also there, presumably because their father was in some particularly inhospitable part of the world. They had to do lessons every morning with a lugubrious tutor who came pedalling down the drive on a bicycle so old-fashioned that it made one think of penny-farthings (to his dismay I used to wreathe it in enormous scarlet poppies to express my glee at being exempt). It was a summer of riding, reading, play-writing, dressing-up, and of not even noticing that Andrew, now at his prep-school, was no longer my chief playmate and closest friend.

I had been allotted the bedroom I loved best, the Corner Room, where I slept in a canopied bed and spent minutes on end studying the huge Pre-Raphaelite engraving above the chimney-piece which showed Christian maidens about to be martyred by Roman centurions. One of the centurions was in love with the most beautiful of the maidens and had taken her aside in order to plead with her to deny her faith. He held her hand, almost in tears, but she had her eyes raised to Heaven, stricken (because she loved him in return) but too noble to give way. The question was: did I want to look, when I grew up, like this maiden, or like one of her companions who, although her robe was less becoming, had longer hair. (Though a fair-skinned, mouse-coloured child, I was determined to have, when I grew up, immensely long and seriously black hair.) The maidens were there in the morning, and at night the smell of the honeysuckle on the terrace came in through the wide-open windows, with the occasional squawk of a moorhen down on the lake, or a volley of quacking from the wild ducks, or the harsh cry of the herons which colonized the nearest island.

These noises seemed to be heard by something inside me rather than by my ears. Like the screeching of the owls, some of them could have been frightening. They were eerie noises, *night* noises: if you hadn't known what made them they would have caused your heart to jump and your scalp to prickle. But I knew them. I had always known them, back through the immemorial length of all my life. They, like the cockling of pheasants before a thunderstorm and the cooing of wood-pigeons and the note of the cuckoo, were the voices of this place. Heard elsewhere, they were only simulacra of themselves; here they were restored to their true nature, as I was to mine.

Once, when I was young enough to share the Corner Room with Andrew, there was an earthquake. That afternoon the sky had gone livid and the grown-ups had said 'There's going to be a thunderstorm – and a good thing too, it'll clear the air.' But there was no thunderstorm. The yellow sky darkened to brown so that the lights had to be switched on, and everyone said 'Extraordinary!' Then bedtime came, I in the canopied bed, he in a little one across its foot. I woke with a jerk because of a roaring noise, and he woke too, saying 'What is it? What is it?!' I said, trying to sound calm, 'It's the thunderstorm.' He was still frightened of thunder but I didn't mind it so much, so I knew I ought to reassure him. 'It isn't thunder,' he said – and I thought 'A very big wind?' Then I realized that the bed and everything else was shuddering – it was the shuddering house that was roaring. Almost at once there were running footsteps in the passage and our mother came in wearing her dressing-gown – it must be the middle of the night. 'You must get up, darlings, it's a little earthquake, we may have to go out in the garden.' But as she spoke, the shuddering stopped. And then there was a silence so huge that it was more frightening than the roaring.

And sure enough, the newspaper said next day that there had been an earthquake, though it was described, annoyingly, as being felt more strongly in Wales.

Once I suffered terrible earache in the Corner Room ('mastoid', they said, and told me afterwards that I had been lucky not to have had an operation; but to my mind an operation would have made it more dignified). That was the first time in my life that I experienced atrocious pain, pain so bad that I rolled myself into a ball in the middle of the bed with the sheet over me like a tent, and one of the grown-ups cried. And once, in that room, when I was so small that Andrew was not yet born, I was in a cot, Mum and Dad in the big bed, and Mum said in a low voice 'Use the slop-pail,' and there was a trickling noise so that I understood that Dad was doing littles – it was amazing that a grown-up should do that. And once Andrew and I invented a game of getting round the same room without touching foot to floor, which involved climbing across the chimney-piece and could only be played secretly because grown-ups would expect us to break things. And over and over again I finished a book which had been interrupted by bedtime, snug under the sheet with a flashlight which had to be hidden quickly if I heard approaching footsteps. Good things were at their best in that room, and bad things were made better by it. Every room I slept in in Gran's house had some special charm about it (except the night nursery, which had a ghost) but the Corner Room was the most interesting of them all.

I called the thing in the night nursery a ghost for want of a better word: it was not like ghosts were supposed to be – more like a monster. I saw it twice, while still young enough to be sat on a pot after breakfast. Because I always took a long time Nanny would leave me there and go back to the day nursery, saying 'Call when you're finished', and I would sit there, bored, feeling the pot's rim engraving a circle round my buttocks. The night nursery looked out over what was called the shrubbery but was nearer to being a little wood – yew trees mostly, and one huge beech which almost curtained the windows, making this room the only gloomily dark one in the house. Sitting on my pot, I would stare out at the leaves of the beech tree, and I was doing this when the 'ghost' appeared.

It was a grey thing like the tip of an elephant's trunk, and it seemed to be groping down towards the outside of the window as though the creature it belonged to were squatting on the roof, reaching down over the gutter. Only a little bit of it appeared at first, withdrawing quickly but riveting my eyes to the place where it had been. Then it came again, more of it, and I screamed. The scream had terror in it, so Nanny came running, but she couldn't understand me when I tried to explain what I'd seen, and ended by telling me that I must have been imagining something; and when I had calmed down I supposed that this was so. Back on my pot next day, I repeated this reassuring explanation to myself: 'I imagined something'. And then I went on to bolster my courage by telling myself that even if I hadn't, the thing was not going to hurt me. It was a *kind* thing, and probably all it ever ate was beech leaves. I so much wanted it not to come – not to be able to come – that I imagined it eating so many beech leaves that it had made itself sick – I even said: '*Poor* thing, it's so sick today that it can't come.' But it did come. It was a much darker grey this time, but it was obviously the same thing and it was *not* kind. I was frantic with fear, and after that I was no longer left alone on my pot in this room. And other people began to say how they had never really liked the night nursery, and that it had a spooky sort of feeling to it.

Some seventy years later I woke one morning in a bed beside a window, and without putting on the glasses which I had worn since I was twelve to remedy my short sight, I looked upwards out of the window to see whether the sky was blue or grey – and there was my 'ghost'. With a tiny tweak of panic, I was back in the night nursery, but only for a split second. This time, though still as short-sighted as ever, I could interpret the grey object: the tail of a pigeon which was perching on the gutter.

The house provided only two other mysterious experiences – minor ones, but at least they remain unexplained. A long time before I was born, my grandfather was sitting one evening in the library and heard a shattering of glass in the dining room next door. He jumped up and ran to the dining room, supposing either that the footman (who ought to have been in bed by that time anyway) had dropped a tray of glasses, or that a burglar, trying to open a window, had slipped and fallen through it. There was nothing amiss, and no explanation of the sound was ever discovered. Not long afterwards my mother was in the Cedar Walk with her dog when she saw the gamekeeper at a distance, through the trees. She started towards him, wanting to give him a message, when her dog suddenly stopped and began to growl and tremble, his hackles rising, staring at where the man was standing. She looked in surprise at the dog, then towards the gamekeeper for an explanation – and there was no one there. My cousin Pen and I liked this story, and sometimes went out after dark hoping to see the Cedar Walk ghost; we used to put on the hooded loden-cloth cloaks which hung in the back passage for everyone's use, as they seemed appropriate wear for such an expedition. But once we were out there in the dark, among the looming cedar trees, it would become only too likely that the ghost really would appear, so we would skedaddle back to the house, singing hymns to ward him off.

The place's other bogeys were purely imaginary, and thus our fear of them something to be ashamed of: the wolves, for example. One Christmas holiday Andrew and I were sleeping on the attic floor, in the Tank Room, so-called because one of its two large built-in cupboards gave access to the water tanks. It was a pleasant room with a sloping ceiling and a relaxed atmosphere, in spite of a spice of danger coming from the tanks' gurglings and the presence in the other cupboard of a lion's head sewn into a dustsheet, which had been left there by some visiting relation and never reclaimed. We liked being up there, but Nanny found it a nuisance, because the room was as far from the nursery as the layout of the house permitted. After nursery tea, when she was getting us washed, brushed and dressed in our prettiest clothes for our hour with the grown-ups in Gran's drawing room, almost always she would find that she had forgotten to bring down a hairbrush or a pair of shoes, whereupon she would say the words I dreaded: 'Run up to the Tank Room and fetch it for me, there's a good girl.' And I would be ashamed to say that I was frightened of the wolves, so off I had to go.

Out through the little 'play-room', a bare ante-chamber to the nursery containing nothing but the toy-cupboard and a canary in a cage on the windowsill, and along the 'green passage': that was all right, because the warmth and sounds of the nursery could still be sensed. Then turn right – tap tap, two steps on bare boards between the humble green carpet and the rich patterned one of the passage which ran like a gallery across the well of the front stairs, onto which the doors of the best bedrooms opened. Here I could have lingered happily, because it was lit by the chandelier hanging over the stairwell and the life of the house rose up like a perfume: a sense of someone writing letters in the library where the fire was dying down (it was allowed to go out when the drawing room fire was lit for the evening); of Gran already in her bright drawing room; of the butler putting away the silver tea things in the pantry;

of Mrs Wiseman, the cook, beginning to prepare dinner in the kitchen. And there were precious things to look at: a chest of carved ivory, a cabinet containing small objects of silver and tortoiseshell, a bowl with huntsmen on stiff-legged horses galloping round it, a cut-glass comport on a little table – very beautiful, but you must be careful not to knock against the table. But if I spent too long dawdling by these things Nanny would wonder what I was doing. I had to go on and turn another corner to the right into the corridor.

The corridor had a high arched ceiling (I thought that all passages with arched ceilings were called corridors), and it was dark. Perhaps I couldn't yet reach the light switch, and even if I could it would only have mitigated the gloom, not dispelled it, because the house's electricity came from a pump down by the stables, and was always dim and fluctuating except in the most important rooms. As soon as I was round the corner into the darkness all the house's sounds were shut off, and the wolves were ahead of me. They lurked in the big best spare-room at the end of the corridor, beyond the point where the stairs sprang up: the 'golden stairs' which we loved in daylight because they *were* golden, of unstained polished oak without a carpet, and spiralled round inside the wall of a tower-like protuberance within an inner angle of the house's U-shape, bisecting two very tall windows as they did so. Anything in the house that was a little odd seemed to us special, but now the slipperiness of these stairs was a worry, because I had to get up them very fast, before I could hear the rattle of claws behind me. It was a desperate scramble, made more desperate by breathlessness, because as soon as I'd turned into the corridor I'd had to start singing as loudly as I could – hymns, of course, like we did in the Cedar Walk – and I mustn't stop for a moment. The ones I knew best were 'While Shepherds Watched' and 'Once in Royal David's City'. I went without pause from the verses I knew of one to those I knew of the other, and back again, and I couldn't stop even when I reached the top of the stairs and got into the Tank Room. It was a little better up there because I could turn on the light, but there was a possibility that one or two of the wolves had slipped ahead of me into the lion cupboard, and anyway the ones that hadn't followed me up the stairs were still waiting at the bottom . . . Not until I had skidded round the corner out of the corridor could I stop singing, draw a long breath, and hear a grown-up's voice saying inside me: '*There* you are – there aren't any wolves at all, you were only imagining them.'

But all this might never have happened, once we were in the drawing room. It was by no means the only time of day when we saw our parents and grandmother. We were in and out of the household's adult life all day, only those of us too young to be able to eat tidily being removed to the nursery for meals (it hung over us for a while as a mild and never executed threat: 'If you can't eat properly you'll have to go back to having lunch in the nursery'). Nurses were there to keep us clean – to mop up babies and chivvy the older ones through their baths and into appropriate clothes – and to air and exercise those of us too young to join in adult walks and rides, not to segregate us. But although 'downstairs' was never forbidden territory, it was only during the hour or so after tea that it was *dedicated to us*.

Then the grown-ups gathered in the drawing room especially for the children's pleasure, and the children became pretty, neat and good-tempered especially for that of the grown-ups. All that shadowed the occasion was its ending. When the drawing room door half-opened and a discreet head poked round it to summon those of us who still had to be put to bed before dinner, then howls would break out: ritual howls, not unpleasant. The grown-ups would indulge them, saying 'Just five more minutes, Nanny, I'll send them up as soon as we've finished this chapter – only three more pages', and there would be mollifying promises of goodnight kisses once we were bathed and in bed. 'After tea' was rarely marred by disharmony.

The drawing room had white walls, pale chintzes, shining furniture of rosewood, walnut and ormolu, ornaments of silver and porcelain, and flowers. Its smell was of freesias, violets, lilies of the

valley, chrysanthemums, daphne. Only when we were older did it
smell of roses – roses were summer, and in summer we would be
out of doors after tea, no one settling in the drawing room until
after the younger children were in bed. Roses in the drawing room
were to belong to growing-up.

The daphne was the most delicious of the drawing room
smells. There were seasons when we might or might not be in the
house, but we were always there at Christmas, when the daphne
was brought in from the greenhouse – there had never been a
Christmas that didn't smell of daphne. It was a special kind
which flourished only for our grandmother: a miniature tree, its
leaves pointed, smooth and yellow-green, its inconspicuous
flowers a faded pink. The scent filled the whole large room,
delicate, sweet, belonging with exquisite intensity to this place
and no other.

When I came into the drawing room I would usually go first to
the flowers. Most of them stood massed on a table with ornate
legs and a sheet of glass on its top, while others in smaller vases
were on the little ormolu-decorated tables on either side of the

*Margaret Carr: 'Gran'*

chimney-piece – a special silver bowl on the table next to Gran's chair was almost always full of Parma violets. I would dawdle round the flower table comparing velvety petals with satiny ones, tangy scents with sweet ones, watching the way in which even the stillest flowers seem minutely to vibrate, dipping nose and lips here and there, and saving the daphne till last. When I breathed it I seemed to be breathing the whole room, the whole house, and my grandmother's love.

We were not allowed to romp in the drawing room – anyone wanting to play rough games could go into the morning room where the furniture was less frail. But we could bring our own toys in if we had become tired of those which lived in the toy-cupboard – those dear, small, battered toys which had served child after child. We could play with those, or at I Spy, or Hunt the Thimble, or spillikins, or dominoes, or cards, or mah-jong, according to age or inclination. But the chief occupation was being read to.

Our ages spanned about twelve years, so if all the cousins were in the house together, as we often were, suitable reading ranged widely. Sometimes *Johnny Crow's Garden* or *Squirrel Nutkin* would be going on, low-voiced, at one side of the fireplace, and *The Thirty-Nine Steps* or *Little Women* on the other; but more often we all listened to the same thing without thought of its being 'too young' or 'too old' for us. We could drift away from or back to the group as we wished, or do something else and listen with half an ear. Old favourites would be relived as they were newly enjoyed by someone younger, the gist of books above one's head absorbed as they were discovered by someone older. *Ivanhoe*, *The Jungle Book*, the *Alice* books, *The Wind in the Willows*, *Struwwelpeter*, *Winnie-the-Pooh*, *What Katy Did*, *Jackanapes*, *Treasure Island*, *The Prisoner of Zenda*, *Peter Rabbit*, *The Princess and the Goblin* – all of them and many others were read to every child, our grandmother's voice weaving its spells back and forth from our babyhood to our adolescence, binding us, without our being aware of it, into a shared experience which extended back from her grandchildren to her children, and sometimes even to her own childhood. Nothing we enjoyed in that house was dearer to us than those evenings, and to this day I can summon up the silky feel of the drawing room carpet as I sat on it contentedly beside Gran's chair.

Carpets were a reliable guide to the standing of the house's inhabitants: precious in the drawing room; handsome in the morning room, library and dining room, and on the front stairs; good in the best bedrooms; becoming plainer and more serviceable as the bedrooms became smaller; changing to linoleum in the nursery, and disappearing altogether on the back stairs and the attic passage onto which the maids' bedrooms opened. There were two back stairs, one from the kitchen to the landing on the first floor which led to the nurseries and the menservants' bedrooms (that wing of the house was only two floors high), and one in the main body of the house rising from the ground floor right to the top. Both were unpolished and uncarpeted, with steep, narrow treads, grey and a bit splintery. Maids could use the golden stairs as well, because they offered the only convenient way between the first and attic floors at that end of the house, but none of them ever set foot on the front stairs except to clean them. In the maids' bedrooms there were squares of old carpet as rugs beside the beds. Getting up on a winter's morning in those rooms was even colder than in the family's rooms – no bedroom was ever heated unless its occupant was ill – because the maids' rooms had only an uninsulated roof above them and draughts whistling up between the floor boards. And the maids had to get up at half-past six, or earlier if there were guests in the house.

There had been a bathroom on their floor since I could remember, but it had not been installed until after I was born. Before that the maids had washed in basins of cold water, as the menservants continued to do – unless, perhaps, the footman went down and fetched hot water for himself and the butler from the kitchen. The men did have a bathroom, but it must have been considered a mistaken extravagance as soon as it was installed, because the tub had never been connected and the room had become a box-room. There was not even a WC for the men, who had to use an outdoor privy in the shrubbery behind the kitchen, which the night nursery overlooked. (This may not have been seen as a great hardship, because my grandfather himself chose to use it after breakfast every morning: if you caught sight of him on his way there, with *The Times* under his arm, you had to pretend you hadn't.) On the other hand, the kitchen, scullery and servants' hall were all warmer than any of the other rooms in the house. No doubt Gran insisted in theory on open windows there, as she did everywhere else, but she rarely went into the kitchen except for the short time each morning when she discussed the meals for the day with Mrs Wiseman, and never into the servants' hall (unless she snooped at night as some of the maids believed, but I don't). We were taught that at least this room and their bedrooms must be private to the servants, and that it was bad manners to intrude; if one of us was sent with a message to the servants' hall we approached it shyly and hesitated before knocking on its door. The sounds coming from behind the door were often cheerful, and the silence which fell when it had been opened, while not quite hostile, suggested a secret life being suspended. We often invaded the kitchen, where Mrs Wiseman would give us a kind welcome and offer titbits, but we were never invited into the hall.

To begin with the servants were the butler and his footman; the cook, her kitchen-maid and her scullery-maid; the head housemaid with her two or three under-housemaids; and Gran's personal attendant – her 'lady's maid'. The coachman (still called that because he dated from before cars, but his successor was called the groom), the chauffeur, the head-gardener and his two under-gardeners all lived outside in their own houses, and so did the old woman with hair-sprouting warts who came to do the washing in the steamy laundry, and spread it to dry in the bleach – a grassy space sheltered by yew hedges.

The work of the junior maids was overseen by their seniors, but they were chosen by my grandmother. Dorothy Morris remembers Gran coming to her family's cottage in 1936 to assess her potential as a kitchen-maid, and taking her on at fifteen shillings a month. Dorothy thought that she had never seen anyone so beautiful, but she also observed that Gran kept a white-gloved hand between her bottom and their horsehair sofa. 'She thinks it may not be clean was my supposition, and I felt some indignation on behalf of my mother, who slaved fiercely to keep the tumbledown place spotless.'

The first butler I can remember was a casting-director's dream for the role: he was called Mr Rowberry, and was tall, bow-fronted and immensely sedate – though he did once make a joke: looking down his nose at an errant puppy, he said: 'They say it's a French poodle, but *I* call it a French puddle,' which struck me as witty beyond words. When his successor retired, the then footman was promoted but was given no footman under him and no livery. He wore a plain dark suit and the children didn't think him a proper butler. That was as far as retrenchment went before the beginning of the Second World War; and it was far enough, in our eyes. Other and much simpler ways of living seemed natural to all of us in other houses, but in this house the way things had always been was the way things ought to be.

When we went up to the attic it was on our way to the roof, or to the dressing-up chest, or to visit Ethel, Gran's lady's maid. She worked up there as well as slept: her pleasant room was a bed-sitting room with a sewing-table, a pigeon-bosomed dressmaker's dummy, and much interesting bric-a-brac. Her photographs and ornaments had stories attached to them, which she liked to tell, and she would give us snippets of material and ribbon. A gentle, sentimental woman, she was affectionate to the little ones and admiring to the older ones, whose dresses she often made; and we were fond of her, partly for her genuine kindness and partly because no one else accepted – or seemed to accept – our superiority so unthinkingly and whole-heartedly. She appeared to *love* 'the gentry' for being what it was.

The dressing-up chest belonged with bad weather – preferably a thunderstorm. There would be the restlessness and uneasiness caused by the heavy feeling of the approaching storm and the unnatural darkening of the air, then the excitement of the crashing thunder, the sudden drumming of rain, gutters filling and spilling, and a scurry in the house as maids ran from room to room shutting the tall sash windows which squealed as they were slammed up or down. Voices would be raised: 'Have you shut the Corner Room? Oh Lord! The garden chairs are out on the terrace.' The house would become a fortress of security and because outdoor activities were so decisively cut off, indoor ones would take on their full significance.

The chest was such a tangle that although we knew everything in it, we always felt that some unfamiliar treasure might emerge. Old evening dresses, satin shoes with cut-steel buckles, lengths of gauze, peasant blouses bought in fits of mistaken enthusiasm on holidays, ribbons, feathers, sequin trimmings, velvet jackets . . . Everything was crushed and smelt slightly musty, and the grown-ups used to laugh and exclaim in dismay at it – 'that *dreadful* old kimono!' – but to us it was all beautiful. We rarely quarrelled over who would wear what. If we were dressing in order to act in a play, choice was dictated by the character one was playing, and if we were dressing for dressing's sake – as we often were – it was almost as strictly dictated by our personalities. One cousin would be aiming for a comic effect, another for something swashbuckling, another for the regal; and the older ones, taking it less seriously than their juniors, would be prepared to sacrifice a cloak or a muslin rose for the sake of peace.

I early and ruthlessly established a claim on what was most romantic, dressing up in order to become a princess or a bride. The trailing, the gauzy, the feathery, the white were what I ferreted out of the heap, with a special preference for veils. My only rival for the romantic was Pen – the others thought me so funny as I teetered about in my princess's raiment that they indulged me. And I could usually defeat poor Pen by the strength of my passion. She would have liked to wear the white velvet bodice and the gauze veil secured by the tinsel crown, but I, once in the mood for dressing-up, *had* to wear them. I thirsted to become what I felt I became in these garments, so much so that even being laughed at failed to weaken their spell. Once, when I was seven, I hit on a headdress which seemed to me inspired. I wanted to be a princess in a twin-horned coif with a veil suspended from the horns – I had seen such a princess in an illustrated history book. There was no such head-dress in the chest, but it came to me that I could take off my knickers and wear them on my head. I was skinny, so the waist-elastic fitted snugly, and the legs stuffed with tissue paper stood up firmly enough as the horns to hold the veil. Although my elders' laughter was fond, I knew perfectly well that it arose from their thinking me absurd, but this had no effect on my own belief in what I had become. I went into a bedroom to look at myself in a long mirror, and I saw myself graceful and beautiful, my face grave under the bloomers, slightly tragic – utterly remote from whatever *they* were seeing. (One day I would be driving along a road in Holland and would catch sight of a grotesque little figure wandering dreamily through an orchard: a child of about seven wearing a pair of her mother's evening shoes, a tattered chiffon dress which trailed in the grass, and a length of white butter-muslin over her head. The whiff I caught of what that child was being almost took my breath away.)

The boys did not dress up, except for plays. Nothing was ever bought for the chest, and women cast off far more clothes than men, so there was little in it with which a boy could express what he wanted to be: no cowboy hats, no bandoleers, no Indian feathers, no weapons. Before being sent to their preparatory schools at the age of eight the boys were subjected to no propaganda about manliness beyond the often disregarded rule that they must be gentle and considerate towards girls, but in two ways, however different the temperaments within the sexes, there was a clear divergence from the start: the girls responded to dress and the boys thought it a bore, and the girls loved horses while the boys were indifferent to them. Being brave was admired regardless of gender, and when we went up on the roof there was nothing to choose between us for daring.

Daring came into it because the point of going up onto the roof was walking round the gutters. The two wings of the house were topped with pitched roofs sloping down to ordinary gutters, but the original part of the house – its main rectangular body – was different. When you climbed up the little stairs next to Ethel's room and unbolted the door at the top of them, you emerged onto a flat field of lead islanded with stout brick chimneys and surrounded by a tiled ridge too high to see over. If you clambered up the inner slope of this ridge and peered over its top, you saw that its steep outer slope, from which dormer windows jutted at intervals, ran down to a flat-bottomed lead gutter almost a foot wide. The idea of sliding down the tiled slope into this gutter at any point between the windows was a little frightening because one would be unable to control the speed of the slide; but if you went down beside one of the windows you had a sort of narrow channel into which to wedge your feet and could find hand-holds on the window, so it became child's play. There would obviously be no problem about walking along that nice wide gutter once you had reached it.

Now that I am old I have a bad head for heights, and it was not too good even in middle age: I remember very disagreeable sensations taking me by surprise when, at the top of a tower somewhere in Italy, I looked down and found that I could see the faraway ground through the open-work iron structure on which I was standing. So ghostly pangs of vertigo now afflict me when I think that once I stood in that gutter, wondering what on earth my mother was fussing about as she stood far below me, clutching her throat in evident anguish while calling up to us to stay quite still – quite *quite* still – until someone had rushed upstairs and opened the window just ahead of us so that we could climb in. So strictly speaking, I suppose, it was not daring that the boys and girls shared in that particular bit of child's play, so much as unawareness of the need for it.

The most important thing about the place, for us children, was its feeling of permanence. It was possible to imagine going away from it, but not possible to imagine its not being there, unchanged, to come back to. This may have been less strongly felt by the grown-ups – only our uncle was young enough to have almost no memory of the time before they lived there – but for us it was what we had *always* known. And if anyone had told us, as we perched on the roof-ridge and looked out over the park, 'This view will cease to exist long before you die', we would have thought him mad. Indeed, much later when I was twenty-two and facing the fact that war had come, I leant my forehead against the trunk of one of the beeches which were such an important part of that view, and comforted myself by saying: 'Well, thank God that whatever happens to us, *you* will still be here when it's over.'

By the end of the war that beech tree had gone. So, very soon afterwards, had the long stand of beeches which rimmed the back park, the noble island of beeches round which the front drive curved, and – most incredible of the lot – the grandest of them all, the huge beech guarding the entrance to the shrubbery behind the rose garden under which I once stood willing my future ghost to inhabit its shade. No person was responsible for their vanishing. Beeches have a lifespan of about two hundred and fifty years, and these, having all been planted at the same time, all died more or less together. Later, Dutch elm disease laid low several other of the park's great beauties, then the most splendid of the cedars was cut down because its roots were threatening the house's foundations, and fierce winds blew down other important trees. Quite gone, now, is the eighteenth-century landscaping of park and garden which used to give the place its charm.

I was once told by a man whose job was looking after the estates of rich people, that one of his dreams was that he would be allowed to sweep away the decaying remains of some great piece of eighteenth-century landscaping, and replant it to a new design. Patching, he said, was useless. Such parks were works of art, and when time destroys them, as it inevitably must, the only right answer is to replace them with another, different, work of art. But who, nowadays, has the money or the vision to plant for the future on a grand scale? He knew that his dream was a crazy one. And certainly in 'our' park the band of quick-growing trees that has now been planted along its edge, between it and the road, although it must have cost a great deal, makes no claim to be landscaping. All it does is shelter the house from view.

How glad I am that it was impossible to imagine the future, and that I had the luck to take – or to mistake – for granted an eighteenth-century landscape just before it fell to pieces, as my natural habitat.

# GOD AND GRAMPS

EVEN IF WALKING the gutters was fun, not brave, courage was considered an important virtue – perhaps not more important than honesty, but more attractive. We knew we ought to be honest, but we wanted to be brave.

Much of this feeling about courage was derived from Geoffrey Salmond, husband of my mother's eldest sister Peggy and father of Joyce, Anne, Pen and John. He was the uncle who ended in the RAF – indeed as head of it. When he was a dashing and amusing young army officer he, with his brother Jack and a small group of friends, became enamoured of that fascinating invention the flying machine, which at that stage appeared to be put together of cardboard and string. They were among the first Englishmen to fly, first as amateurs, soon afterwards as members of the Royal Flying Corps, which they got going. Early in the First World War Geoff played an important part in persuading the War Office that airborne men would be invaluable at finding out what was going on behind the enemy's lines – he was one of the Flying Corps thinkers, as well as a daring pilot. After the war he made the first ever flight across the Himalayas, when navigation was a matter of peering earthwards and following rivers and (when there were any) roads. He also became the commander of the RAF in India, and contributed a good deal to the development of civil aviation.

His adoring wife understood from the beginning that on no account must she betray how much she feared for him when he was flying: if you were married to a hero it was your duty to be heroic too, and never to burden him with an image of yourself being unhappy for fear of losing him. She played her part to perfection: all their lives her daughters would remember how proudly their father told them that she was 'as brave as a lion'.

She was to need this courage, poor Aunt Peggy. First Geoff died of bone cancer when he was only middle-aged, then their son John, who had followed his father into the RAF, was killed in the Second World War. I did not see her under the immediate impact of these two terrible blows, but I know what got her through them: the conviction that to give way would be unworthy of Geoffrey Salmond's wife. She and her daughters, although they never spoke of it, were always thereafter to have about them a faint aura of dedication to an inspiring memory. They were examples of the valuable aspect of that Good Behaviour so well understood by the novelist Molly Keane.

It is an ideal that can, of course, be damaging. Once, when my mother was eighty, the husband of a good friend of hers died suddenly, and when I arrived for a weekend two days later she told me about it with feeling, knowing how deeply her friend would feel her loss. I said 'Oh God, I must call her'; and when I had done so my mother muttered in a shamefaced way 'How brave you are.' – 'Brave?' – 'She might have cried.' It turned out that she had not yet dared to get in touch with her friend: a fear of raw emotion that can cripple human responses, as well as support endurance.

When we were children there were, of course, no undercurrents to being brave. It was just a stylish way to behave, at which the Salmonds were a good deal better than I was. I was well aware that if we were faced with a really hairy jump in cold blood, Pen would be much readier than I to put her pony at it; anyone could be brave out hunting because of the excitement, but she was always brave. From time to time it worried me: in a situation which required real heroism – if someone was drowning in a turbulent river, perhaps, or trapped in a burning house – would I be able to rise to the occasion? It didn't feel likely, but on the other hand it was possible that nobody felt it likely – that given such a situation you responded in the right way either automatically, or because you were so frightened of what people would think if you didn't that doing it was the lesser evil. I could only hope . . .

We knew the Bible well – or rather, those parts of it read to us by Gran, starting when we were very young: Joseph and his brethren, Samson and Delilah, David and Jonathan, Samuel and Eli, Christ walking on the water, the miracle of the loaves and fishes, and of course the story of Jesus's birth. Gran read or told those stories as though they were about real events which were parts of everyone's knowledge and life. She loved most of the books she read to us, but she loved the Bible best: the Old Testament stories, particularly, she told with contained relish. She introduced us to poetry only through narrative verse, chiefly Macaulay's and Scott's, but it was to poetry more broadly speaking that she led us through the Bible, by the vibration of her response to it. To poetry, rather than to morality, in that it made little impression as a source of a sense of right and wrong.

My grandparents were sensible and modest people, so I doubt that either of them would have presumed to claim that he or she was a *good* Christian, but equally I am sure neither of them doubted that Christians they were. They were regular churchgoers; they respected the Sacraments; they obeyed the Ten Commandments; they felt strongly – even passionately – that faith should be drawn as directly as possible from the Bible without the intervention of a priesthood (hence their detestation of Roman Catholics). But if they actually *believed* in the Incarnation, which I take to be Christianity's central tenet, their conduct concealed the fact. It seemed much more like the conduct of people moved by common sense combined with an ideal of gentlemanly behaviour than it did like the conduct of people seeking communion with God.

What people like them would have said in response to such a thought was that a person's beliefs – his really important, inner beliefs – were a matter between himself and God, too important to be lightly exposed. About which I feel doubtful. It seems to me more likely that what could not be lightly exposed was a person's really important inner disbelief.

As far as I was concerned, they gave me an extraordinarily undemanding God. It was His love and His understanding that were emphasized, so much so that I found it cheering, not alarming, to remember that He knew everything about me: every thought, every motive, every illegitimate desire. Because He knew every single thing, and understood it, then He knew the strength of temptations and how, considering my frailty, I didn't do too badly against them. People might misunderstand, He wouldn't. Whatever tensions there were (and there were some), the bedrock of trust had not been cracked: what I expected from life and from God was love, forgiveness and protection. I was threatened only if naughty or silly, and then, however resentful I might feel at the moment, I knew well enough that it was my own fault, and I needed to call on no great moral energy to accept that fact. This was because most of the sins committed by me and the other children didn't matter very much to anyone and certainly not to God. The only sin taken really seriously was the one which, if you brought it off successfully, would make nonsense of adult control: lying.

The dreadfulness of lying was brought home to me when I was four years old. All the family's children were at a tea party in a neighbour's garden, where there was a cherry tree trained against a wall: overwhelmingly tempting because cherries were rare in our county and their smooth redness was so perfect. They were, in fact, the bitter kind grown for jam-making, but I was unaware of that as I gazed longingly, feeling in anticipation the protective net's fine thread as I pushed fingers through it, the slight harshness of the leaves, the plumpness of the fruit. I didn't dare, though. This was Cousin Minnie's garden, not ours, and she was proud of her cherries. But I was hand in hand with my cousin Anne, four years my senior, who was showing me how to play hide-and-seek properly, and who was touched by my expression. 'We oughtn't to,' she said – and then, generously: 'Look, *I* mustn't because I know that it's wrong, but *you* can have just one.' So I took the cherry she picked for me, bit into it, let it drop because of its unexpected sharpness, clutched at it – and squashed it against the front of my frock. There in the middle of my stomach was a large red stain, advertising my theft for all the world to see.

My consternation was so great that I didn't howl, only stared appalled at my cousin. Hers was even greater. She was a redhead of remarkable untidiness, her socks always wrinkled round her ankles, her bloomers always showing under her skirt, always longing to do right and ending by doing wrong. A clown and a tragedienne, she laughed and cried with abandon, loved to act and to tell stories, rejoiced in ideas of nobility, self-sacrifice and daring. The person she would most have liked to have been was the Boy who Stood on the Burning Deck – a poem which she often declaimed. She was adored by us, the younger ones, because of her loving kindness and her entertainment value; and now I knew at once that she would shoulder the responsibility for my sin.

And sure enough, 'Don't cry,' she said. 'It's all my fault and I know what we'll do. We'll run home very quickly and I'll wash your dress, and by the time they all get back they won't be able to see any stain and no one will know.'

It was easy to leave the garden by a back way without anyone seeing, and then we only had to cross a lane to be in the park of my grandparents' house. 'Faster, faster!' cried Anne, becoming the Red Queen, and I was whirled along like Alice in the picture. Anne had an inkling that the disappearance of two members of the tea party, one of them only four, would cause alarm. I didn't think of this or anything else, having simply become part of a situation compounded of urgency and secrecy out of which I was about to be miraculously delivered. We covered half a mile of park and garden at high speed, pausing sometimes to gasp and clutch at the stitches in our sides, crept up to and into the house, and bolted into a bathroom. 'Quick, quick, undress – look, I'll run the bath – if they come I'll say I'm giving you your bath and it won't be a lie because you'll be in it.'

No sooner was I in the bath and the stained frock in the hand-basin than there came a rattling at the door. 'Are you in there?' 'What are you doing? Open the door at once – what are you *doing*?' My mother's voice was agitated – the adults had had time to suppose that the older child had fled in panic at some disaster overtaking the younger one. The bedraggled frock came out of the basin with the stain still there – it was no good saying 'I'm giving her her bath' with the evidence glaring. Anne had one last inspiration: 'Sh!' she whispered, 'I'll pretend I'm going to the lav,' and she whipped down her knickers, sat on the pan and began to grunt with conscientious realism. I sat in the chilly water (there had been no time to adjust the temperature), as quiet as a mouse, overcome by the daring of this last device, and still trusting my protector's ingenuity.

'I *know* you aren't just going to the lavatory,' cried my mother (how? What hope against these guilt-detecting eyes which would see through doors?); 'Let me in AT ONCE!' And when the door was opened at last and the tearful confession had been made, it turned out – and this was amazing – that stealing the cherry hadn't been a sin at all, nor even had staining the dress. It was, explained my mother, *the lie* that had been so very wrong. But I had never *said* I hadn't stolen the cherry – surely lies were *words*? But no: it appeared that a lie could be something as complex and exhausting as running all the way across the park and sneaking into the house and pretending to have a bath. It was a cheering thought, once absorbed, because it proved that hiding sins was much more trouble than admitting them; and I have never since then been much of a liar. Excepting on those very rare occasions when the absolute necessity for it has been so overwhelming that it didn't feel like lying at all.

Which must, I suppose, have been the case with my grandfather – the apparently impeccable source of his household's wholesome atmosphere – when his only son, while still an undergraduate at Oxford, announced that he wished to become engaged to a young woman who was a Roman Catholic. This comic recurrence of crisis at Oxford, which seems to have become almost a tradition, was something that none of us knew about until recently, when it turned up in another old suitcase crammed with letters kept by my grandmother.

My grandparents had never met the young woman, who lived in the north of England with her aunt – perhaps she was an orphan. How my uncle met her is not revealed, but they had known each

*William Greenwood Carr: 'Gramps'*

other well for two years: this is stated in the first of the letters, from the young woman's aunt to my grandfather, which protests in courteous and reasonable terms at his forbidding the engagement without ever having met her niece. She says that the two young people know each other well, that the attachment between them is sincere, and that her niece is a good and sensible girl as well as a charming one, and does not deserve a dismissal so sudden and cruel. She goes on to say that while she agrees with him in theory that it is best if husband and wife are of the same faith, she must point out that she herself is a Protestant who has been married to a Roman Catholic for thirty years without any problems, so she can assure him from her own experience, as well as that of other couples of her acquaintance, that a 'mixed marriage' is not by any means necessarily disastrous. She is not asking – she says – that he reverse his decision at once, but she does feel that it would be only fair for him and his wife to meet her niece before finally forbidding the engagement.

The second letter is my grandfather's answer, in the form of a copy made in my grandmother's hand. It is brusque. Even, he says, if the young woman is foolish enough to wish to become engaged to an idle and frivolous young man who has so far shown no inclination whatever to earn a living, her aunt must surely see that it is her duty to forbid it, given that his estate happens to be entailed in such a way that his son, if he marries a Roman Catholic, will never inherit a penny. End of letter. And end, obviously, of engagement. *And my grandfather was lying*: no such entail existed.

It gives me great satisfaction to report that as soon as my grandfather was dead – he died in his sixties, while his son was still quite young – my uncle, who could always get whatever he wanted from a doting mother, married not only a Roman Catholic, but an Italian Roman Catholic – a veritable emissary from the Scarlet Woman of Rome. For that was what low-church Protestants of my grandparents' generation felt 'papists' to be.

At first that lie of my grandfather's made me laugh. On consideration it is not funny. Many an Ulsterman has become a murderer because he did not feel that ridding the world of a Catholic – or a Protestant, as the case might be – counted as murder. To him the act of murder feels righteous: the end has justified the means, as preventing his son from marrying a Catholic seemed to my grandfather to justify his lie. In both cases the humanity of the victim has been obscured by what the murderer and the liar feel to be an overwhelming necessity.

It is often said of monstrous evils such as genocide that we must not let ourselves forget them because the potential for such crimes lurks in all of us. I have said it myself, thinking that it must be true – but secretly I have never been able to *feel* that it is true of me. Now, however, having seen the obvious link between my grandfather's attitude to Catholics and that of Protestants in Northern Ireland, I have to acknowledge that I was led to it by seeing the link between my own few felt-to-be necessary lies and my grandfather's . . . There is a connecting thread there, between the almost harmless use of a psychological mechanism which can be brought into play when a need for self-justification is felt, and an evil use of it. Hugely different though the ends may be, the mechanism is the same. This kind of discovery must, I suppose, be the central reason for trying to write the truth, even if indecent, about oneself.

If you no longer lied, you were left with all those nice little sins than which lying was so much worse. It was wrong to steal grapes from the vinery, peaches from the kitchen-garden wall, lump sugar from the fat white jars in Gran's store cupboard. It was wrong to slide down haystacks in such a way that the stack was damaged and rain could get into the hay. It was wrong to scatter the grain heaped in the granary by wading through it. It was wrong to leave gates open so that cattle could stray. It was wrong to neglect an animal for whom one was responsible. Some of these rules, like the ones about animals and (later) the one about never pointing a gun at anyone even if it wasn't loaded, we never thought of breaking because that would be improper behaviour in our own eyes. Others we broke constantly because the forbidden pleasures were irresistible. Our awareness of the 'sinfulness' of these wrongdoings came from our own need for excitement, rather than from outside.

There were also, of course, aspects of one's own behaviour that one knew grown-ups would disapprove of such as our early interest in excretion and (from the age of ten or eleven, in my case) an eagerness to discover everything possible about sex. But those were so private that they didn't feel like sins – though whether this was because even God couldn't know about them, or because of His understanding, I can't now remember.

Sometimes a sin was discovered unexpectedly: who would have guessed it was sinful to organize a church service in an unoccupied spare bedroom on a Sunday when colds had prevented us from going to church? This was during a short period of religious fervour when I was about ten. It was Anne and her elder sister who thought of it, and who insisted on secrecy in case our service might amount to the mysterious sin of taking God's name in vain. 'It will only be all right' I was told severely, 'if *all* of us are absolutely sincere.' That was fine: I felt tremendously sincere. A glow of virtue flooded me, and I was smugly aware of God's surprised pleasure at our piety.

Unfortunately Anne decided to write the numbers of the hymns we would sing on cards and stick them up as though in a real church, and while doing so upset a bottle of Indian ink on a white counterpane . . . clear proof that we didn't have God's approval, even before the frightful moment when Hannah, the head housemaid, came in to see what all the whispering and giggling was about, and discovered the blotch.

Piety was often connected with our grandfather, because he had died. One morning, when I was six, we had all been made to sit quietly in the morning room while my mother read to us – an unusual event at that time of the day, but agreeable. Suddenly, from upstairs, there came a scream. It was a sound so foreign to our experience that we didn't quite believe we had heard it. Mum put down the book, stared into space for a few seconds, then got up and went out of the room without saying a word. Later that day Nanny took us out for a walk, and as we passed the front of the house I noticed that all three windows of the room in which Gramps had been lying ill were wide open. I asked why, and Nanny hushed me. Coming back from the walk we met Gran, who was going down to the stable-yard to feed her doves, as she always did. She looked tired. Before Nanny could stop me I ran up to her and asked 'Why are all Gramps's windows open?' – 'He's not there any more, my darling,' Gran said, her face full of sorrow and tenderness. 'He's gone away to Heaven to be with God.' The windows must have been open so that his soul could fly out of them. Later, it was a disappointment to learn I was too young for funerals. I longed to see the team of Suffolk Punches taking him to the church on one of the farm wagons, specially decked out for the occasion, and even more, to see Susan being led along behind. She was the little black hackney he always drove when he went to Norwich, who whizzed him along so fast that they covered the twelve miles in less than an hour.

Being with God made Gramps – in life a distant figure, presumably benign but never cosy – more approachable. He blended with God, and there was a time during the pious period when I felt that my prayers would be more effective if I said them in the room where he died. It took courage to go into that room (the one where the wolves used to lurk, now reverted to being the very best spare-room, too grand for children to sleep in), and even more courage to kneel down at the foot of the stately four-poster. I said the Our Father, and waited. The holiness in the room and the holiness in my heart seemed to swell, and to be about to merge – the sensation was almost physical – and Gramps's (or God's) presence, so earnestly hoped for to begin with, began to loom . . . Both times I did this my nerve failed, and I crept out of the room knowing I was a coward in giving up before what might have been going to happen actually did so.

The only time Gramps's spirit did intervene, it was in a manner both practical and kind. On a summer Sunday, when for some reason Pen and I had not been taken to church, we were left in charge of the dogs. If they were not shut up (which no one could bear to inflict on them) these dogs, not the gun-dogs but the family's pets, would disappear on hunting expeditions whenever they got a chance. It was a really bad sin to let the dogs go hunting, because they disturbed the game which enraged keepers, fathers and uncles, and they also risked getting stuck down rabbit-holes or caught in traps, which appalled everyone. The worst offender was Lola, Gran's poodle, a sober little dog of impeccable behaviour except that she was a devil for hunting, took with her any other dog who happened to be there, and would sometimes stay out for several days and nights during which everyone fretted and mourned.

On this Sunday we took several volumes of old *Punches* and climbed into the 'spreading-tree', an ancient larch trained into the shape of a table and propped on wooden supports. Easy to climb into, fragrant and feathery, it offered places where its twigs interlaced to form hammocks. Much time was spent in it, and much time was spent studying old *Punches*.

These – many volumes of them – lived behind the sofa in the morning room. Sometimes I sat on the floor in the cosy narrows between bookshelf and back of sofa, and looked at them there; but they were not the precious kind of book which had to be handled delicately, so could be lugged off wherever you wished. They were not for reading – the narrow columns of tiny type, so small that instead of looking like blackness on whiteness it gave the impression of foggy greyness, were too off-putting. It was the pictures with their rambling captions which fascinated me. I liked best the ones with horses in them – and most nineteenth-century outdoor scenes included horses – and the ones of handsome Edwardian ladies drawn by du Maurier, whose dresses I admired. The earlier ladies, in crinolines sometimes so huge that they got stuck in doorways, were funny but not so appealing (Gran said that she and her sisters used to despise girls who wore huge crinolines and laced their corsets so tightly that they fainted; and indeed, the only crinoline in the dressing-up chest was a modest one). It didn't occur to me that *Punch* was better than history books, but it was: it didn't seem to be about anything as abstract as 'the Past', just about how things used to be.

That day, up in the spreading-tree, the *Punches* were as absorbing as ever. When the family came back from church . . . no dogs.

Lunch would be served in a few minutes, but still neither of us felt it unjust when they rounded on us and said: 'Go out and find them, and don't come back until you have.' In tears, but unresentful, we set off through the park towards the bridge and weir simply because we had been shooed in that direction, our bare legs swished by the long grasses of summer. The dogs wouldn't still be in the park – Lola was too serious for the mild sport offered there – and it was only too possible that they had crossed the bridge into the woods stretching on either hand on the far side of the lake. When we reached the bridge the proliferation of potential directions overwhelmed us. We stood there, calling feebly 'Lola! Jeanie! Tarry!' knowing they were probably out of earshot by now, and wouldn't answer to being called anyway. Guilt and hopelessness combined, and we wept again.

'We'd better try the sand-field,' said Pen, two years my senior and, like her sister Anne, more given to virtue and self-sacrifice than I was. The sand-field, so-called for its light soil, adjoined the park and had a large rabbit population. When we scrambled through the hedge we saw that none of the rabbits were about: a hopeful sign – they might have gone to earth because the dogs had passed this way. We agreed that it was worth going on, and started towards the gap in the far hedge where once a gate had hung.

This gap was now full of a tall green growth, and we could soon see what it was: stinging-nettles. The hedge was impenetrable and the nettles merged at each side with its undergrowth of brambles. There was no path through, and the nettles stood as tall as us. Any adult would have walked up to the top of the field and round into the next one by another way, but we had become hypnotized by our impossible task and were capable of seeing no solution but going back home or going straight on. It was hot, we were hungry, the nettles smelt rank and were full of midges. 'We *can't* get through,' I sobbed; but Pen, on whom the situation was working differently, said: 'We must. We must pray.'

'To God, or to Gramps?' I asked.

'To both – and you must *really mean it.*'

'Shall we kneel down?'

No, said Pen, to kneel down out of doors would be showing-off. It would be enough if we shut our eyes and put our hands together. Even so, I felt uncomfortably exposed in the tense silence of our praying. 'Please, please God, and please Gramps, don't let the nettles sting me – us – and let the dogs be on the other side.'

Pen went first, silent but steady, her hands still together. I had a track to follow, but still the hairy leaves brushed my legs and arms, and sometimes even my neck. They might have been buttercups. So astounded were we when we reached the other side, both unstung, that we were unable to speak, and we were not surprised, only awestruck when we looked out over the field to see two of the dogs circling a clump of brambles, and earth dug by Lola showering out of its centre.

We took the dogs back by a different route, didn't talk about our miracle, and never tempted God or Gramps by asking for another. Partly this was because the pious fit was evaporating anyway, partly

it was because we were scared. Whatever powers we had touched
in Heaven or ourselves, we felt that nettles ought to sting.

What brought us to heel morally far more effectively than talk of
Right and Wrong was the word that had such remarkable potency
in our family: silly. It was the word most often used by grown-ups
when they were scolding, and it worked so well because while
'naughty' or 'bad' added drama to a situation, and even hinted at
forces which might be beyond your control, 'silly' was something
you could easily be (very likely had been, in whatever was the case
in point); and silliness was, or you felt it ought to be, within your
control. It was a maddening, snubbing little word, and you often
raged against it, but in the end it contributed a great deal to giving
us the idea that people are responsible for their own actions, and
ought to be prepared to accept their consequences. Far more than
God, up there in His marvellous world of all-embracing love, and
of magic, it belonged to the world we understood.

# PAIN

THERE WAS, of course, pain, and pain of a kind more serious than that caused by the puzzles and humiliations of being young. Ours came from unhappiness between our parents.

Mothers were more important than fathers because fathers were often away, even when not posted overseas: and ours, though kind, was squeamish. He had a phobia about vomiting, so the ease with which babies spill their contents made him wary of us in our infancy. I know how powerful this revulsion can be because I have shared it, and for many years, if I had the misfortune to see or hear someone throwing up I would feel ill all day and for months afterwards whenever I chanced to recall it. I was eventually cured (more or less) by having from time to time to look after someone ill: in those circumstances, I could, by making a tremendous effort, overcome the phobia. But Dad never had to nurse anyone, so he was always afflicted by it, and it is possible that subconsciously he continued to see us, until we were safely grown-up, as creatures who *might* give him a horrible experience. He gave only the most dutiful of goodnight pecks and never hugged or stroked us.

We enjoyed him when he was funny, as he often was – indeed, on the only occasion he read to us he made it so tremendously funny that it was a new kind of experience, and I was disappointed that he never read to us again. We were happy to share jokes with him: for instance the *Who-is-Captain-of-this-ship-I-AM* that had to be shouted to stop a dithering argument about what we were going to do – the first person to get it out won, and it was usually but not always him. And he was brilliant at remembering comic songs. We – or at least I – knew that he was a very nice man. Nevertheless, we mirrored his lack of physical warmth. And, what is more, I have never in my life been attracted to a man of his physical type: fair-haired, blue-eyed, pink-skinned. And my brother once told me that when he was a boy he found Dad repulsive.

How could a trim man with pleasant features, an unusually agreeable nature and a lively sense of humour have become repulsive? It was a fate laid down for him long before he met her by his wife's mother, my beloved Gran.

Gran believed that no lady could want to be kissed by a man unless she truly loved him enough to marry him; and that no gentleman would dream of trying to kiss a lady unless he truly loved her enough to propose marriage. And this belief she handed down to her daughters. In most families there are both accepters and rejecters of parental beliefs, but in this one all the daughters turned out to be accepters (one of them found it impossible quite to fit in, but she blamed herself for it and did her gallant best to make up for it). Certainly my mother, the youngest, although spirited and full of *joie de vivre*, cheerfully accepted what her adored mother had taught her.

When she was nineteen, early in the second year of the First World War, she went to a dance and met a young army officer who had been invalided home from the front. Her friends all liked him, he was easy to talk to, and he loved country things as much as she did. He fell in love with her on sight, and before the evening was out had kissed her in the conservatory – and she had thoroughly enjoyed being kissed. It was the most exciting thing that had ever happened to her. My father was one of those gentlemen who would not have kissed a lady unless he had truly fallen in love with her, so very soon afterwards he asked her to marry him. Naturally she said yes. She knew she liked him, but more than that: she was sure she couldn't possibly enjoy being kissed so much if she didn't love him. It did not occur to her that lively girls enjoy being kissed because being kissed is fun.

Whether my father was a virgin, as my mother certainly was, I

*Mum and Dad's wedding day, 1916*

do not know, but I am sure that if he was not, it was by only a very narrow margin. He was a clergyman's son who had gone from his public school straight to the Royal Military Academy at Woolwich, and who – four years before meeting my mother – had received the following letter from the man about to be his commanding officer in the regiment he was joining straight from the Academy. And – more to the point – he was going to keep that letter all his life as an inspiration.

. . . I make section commanders very independent and make them entirely responsible for their men, horses, barrackrooms and discipline, as far as possible. I expect them to know their men and horses intimately, and see to their clothing, kits and all details of the equipment in the gun park, and to be good instructors in gunnery and musketry, riding and driving drills, and a friendly adviser to them in all other matters.

In the same way I expect my officers to come to me whenever in difficulty, official or private affairs, as I make myself responsible for them. A smart, keen officer makes, by example, smart, keen NCOs and men. In matters of duty one cannot be too particular, and I hold that supervision over an officer, to see whether he performs his duty or not, should never be required. An officer holding the King's Commission should never require supervision in the routine of his duty. He does his work whether seen or unseen as a gentleman, and 'plays the game' in spirit as well as letter in accordance with his C.O.'s desires. Play up for those under you whom you serve, and the result spells success in the Army for a man of ability.

Bad language and an overbearing manner does not get good work out of anyone. The Briton can be easily led but is a tough man to drive. Leading not driving is the system.

On parade I am your C.O. and expect soldierlike smartness in every action and address. Off parade I hope to be your instructor and adviser and companion in all field sports and pastimes. This letter I fear is rather of the nature of a 'jaw' but I thought it better to let you know what to expect.

I know you are a keen sportsman, and will stretch points to give you leave for hunting, shooting, fishing, football, cricket etc, but I do not care about 'racing men' and the class of people who go off to loaf about in Town. There is plenty of sport here to fill up all your time. We have a regimental pack of harriers – the subscription to it is five shillings a month in winter and two and sixpence in summer. Two afternoons a week we meet and you can gallop to your heart's content – but you must look after your horses on return! The Tidworth Foxhounds are also handy. There is football and hockey galore.

A keen sportsman usually makes the best soldier. He learns to acquire an 'eye for a country' and to keep himself fit, deny himself luxuries to take part in sport, and obtains a knowledge of men and manners which cannot be learnt elsewhere. He keeps himself morally and physically fit and those are the conditions requisite to enable him to learn instruction in soldiering.

To turn to other matters – you can have a good horse from Government for £10 a year, and this will probably be enough to commence with. If another is within your means (and I should like to hear from your people on the subject) no doubt we can pick up a cheap one for £30 or £40. The additional horse would cost you about £3 a month. As regards kit – a good hunting saddle and bridle (Sowters for choice) and a secondhand saddle from Parkers in St Martin's Lane (or elsewhere) and an exercising snaffle bridle. Bandages and a fawn rug with your initials on it (from the Stores) will set you up in horse kit except for a few odds and ends you can get from Battery stores.

As regards kit – a dark grey hunting frock coat which can be worn with a pot hat and butcher boots, and tan-coloured breeches, make a good harrier hunting kit. Daniells has our regimental hunt button, but if you want to do things cheaply go to Moss, 21 King Street, Covent Garden for the grey frock coat – he also has our hunt button which of course should be *black* ones, not brass. Later on, as you come along, we can think about white breeches and top boots and a top hat for foxhunting.

When fellows can mount themselves decently and go decently they are allowed to blossom out into a 'pink' coat, but there is plenty of time for that! Hunting kit is an economy as people cannot hunt in walking clothes. It ruins them and they look horrible and serve no purpose afterwards.

Butcher boots with soft legs and black tops look well, but plain butcher boots are good enough. Bartley makes the best boots, but old Craig and Davis are cheaper and can make a decent boot for many people.

A short hunting crop and brown leather thong. I get mine from near Weedon – Sharpe, Whipmaker, Flore, Weedon – and have them made 22 inches long. He is a cheap man.

In other matters write to me, and I will tell you what to do.
You can send this letter on to your people in case they want
any further information about your future surroundings.
. . .Yours sincerely.

D. G. Geddes

It is clear that any young man to whom D. G. Geddes stood *in
loco parentis* would need to be determinedly dissident if he wanted
to 'loaf about in Town' – which meant, of course, pursue the
company of women, to say nothing of gaining sexual experience of
them; and my gentle and honourable father was not even slightly
dissident by nature.

My mother had been told nothing about sex, except that she
might not at first like the thing men wanted to do, but would
get used to it. The only criticism of her mother I ever heard her
utter, almost a lifetime later, was that it had been wrong of her
not to overcome her embarrassment and say more. My mother's
honeymoon came – as it did to many brides of her generation – as
a shock.

Just before the war she had been sent abroad to a 'finishing
school', as was the custom in her sort of family: it was a way of
keeping girls at 'the awkward age' (we would say teenagers)
occupied. Smart people chose Paris, but Switzerland or Germany
seemed less risky to most parents, so my mother's lot was Dresden
and included exposure to a certain amount of Wagner which she
described in a letter home as 'lovely of course, but very long and
very noisy'. Another letter, addressed to a sister, is headed NOT
TO BE SHOWN TO ANYBODY NOT EVEN MOTHER, and
starts 'I say not even Mother because I am going to be vulgar and
I don't want darling little Mother to know how vulgar I can be.'

She then tells how, when she was out with other girls for an
evening stroll chaperoned by Mademoiselle, she saw approaching
under the lime trees a group of hussars, and soon realized that one
of them was gazing at her with alarming intensity. His gaze held her
throughout his approach, and as they passed each other his head
swivelled as though her face had magnetized his eyes. She blushed

scarlet 'from head to foot', and as she walked on she prayed that when the hussars reached the end of the promenade they would leave it, not turn round as Mademoiselle and her charges would do, to walk back. But no sooner had the girls started their return than she saw the hussars coming towards her again, and again he was gazing at her. And this time, when they passed each other, she (though still blushing furiously) lifted her eyes to meet his – and smiled! End of vulgarity.

Not much happened to increase her sophistication between then and her marriage. The discovery of what she was expected to do in bed with her husband threw her. She was a healthily passionate girl, but passion collided with ignorance so disastrously that the connection between the deliciousness of being kissed and the sexual act was broken. Full sex was not just disappointing, it was embarrassing and horrid. And my father – inexperienced, shy about physical demonstrations of affection, and probably ashamed of his own sexual impulses – was far from being able to prove her wrong. He was particularly at a disadvantage because it had not been *him* to whom she had responded so eagerly when he kissed her, only the fun of being kissed: he was not, physically, the type of man to whom she was drawn.

She did get used to it, and the first years of their marriage went reasonably well, helped by his being away a good deal, then by her being pregnant with me, and then, immediately after the war's end, by their sharing the adventure in Abyssinia – though that was rather spoilt by the beginning of her second pregnancy. But soon after my brother's birth she met a man – one of my father's fellow-officers – with whom she discovered what being in love and making love were really like, and that was the end of any attempt on her part at married happiness.

It was not, however, the end of the marriage. Her parents found out that she was having an affair: found out through the agency of the same sister to whom she had reported smiling at the hussar. That sister, though asked not to show the letter to anyone, NOT EVEN MOTHER, had promptly done just that, as was proved by my finding it in Gran's collection of all the letters she had ever

received from her daughters. 'She always was a sneak,' said my
mother, aged eighty-five – and so indeed she was. On a visit to
London in about 1922 this sister was waiting for a friend in the hall
of the University Women's Club, of which Mum was a member,
when my mother swept in accompanied by an unknown man,
looking so radiantly beautiful that for a moment she was not
recognizable. What was said I do not know, but when my aunt got
home next day she reported to their father: 'Kitty is having an
affair.'

My aunt told me this herself, when I was driving her back from
London to Norfolk one day, and why she told me I have never been
able to work out. She was always slightly given to little paroxysms
of confession, but this was not little, and nothing led up to it: we
had just been laughing at some extravagance of my mother's when
she suddenly said: 'Oh, poor Kit – I once did such a terrible thing
to her, I could never tell you what it was.' Naturally I protested that
to say so much without saying more was unforgivable, and – not
very unwillingly – she gave way. What happened then, she said, was
that Gramps wrote to my mother saying that unless she broke with
this man at once the family would never see her again, my father
found this letter in my mother's handbag, and my mother had a
nervous breakdown and had to go into a nursing-home for a 'sleep-
cure'.

Poking about in her handbag is so unlike my father that at first
I found it hard to believe. But if the letter arrived by the first post,
at breakfast time, and she opened it in front of him – 'Oh, look, a
letter from Dad' . . . The shock would have been undisguisable, she
would almost have fainted, would certainly have had to leave the
room with it as fast as possible. And even if it didn't happen like
that, there were other ways in which he could have known that the
letter had come, then seen her dismay. And although he was not a
particularly observant man, it seems likely that someone whose wife
was so lit-up by an affair that her own sister had almost failed to
recognize her, would already have had an inkling that something
was up. My father may well have been in a tormented state for
weeks, struggling to believe that his suspicions were unfounded, so

that her reaction to her father's letter was the last straw.

'Sleep-cures' were popular during the twenties: the patient was sedated so heavily for several days that she was oblivious of whatever was done to her in the way of nourishment and evacuation (it sounds delicious).

I don't know whether my parents discussed divorce, but I doubt it. If my mother had got divorced she would have been cast out by her parents (perhaps, in the end, not; but she would have been convinced that this would happen at the time) and would have lost her children: it is improbable that my father, who truly loved her, could have borne inflicting all that on her, and certain that she would not have demanded it. Even if her lover was in a position to marry her – and I have no idea whether he was – I think she was too much a daughter to face the prospect of losing her parents in any circumstances, and probably too much a mother (though less so than she would later become) to face losing us.

From then on she *knew* that she loathed being touched by my father, although her guilt prevented her from entirely denying him his 'rights'. To continue having sex, even if only occasionally, with someone whose touch has become hateful, is nerve-racking; while on his side, poor man, to be unable to resist making love to someone you adore, even though you know she can hardly bear it, is misery. So the quarrels began – not, or not publicly, about what was really wrong, but about an endless series of little things: his unpunctuality, her extravagance, whether to do this or that, whether to go here or there . . . It became impossible for them to be together for more than two days running without there being a row, almost always started by her. There was never any physical violence worse than flouncing out of rooms and banging doors, but the emotional disturbance was acute.

It was only after my father's death that I learnt (again from letters) how sad and patient he had been. As soon as the Second World War began he had returned to the Army, and had the good fortune to be sent to Ethiopia to run an officers' training corps for Haile Selassie (he could speak Amharic – in fact he was probably the only officer in the British Army who could). This was a quirky kind of occupation that suited him – he became known for communicating with his headquarters by means of homing pigeons, which he trained. But the process of demobilization took a long time to reach him at his exotic outpost – a pink palace at Harar – and he was feeling pretty homesick by the time he wrote to my mother to tell her he would soon be back. It is distressing to know that he then, so many years after their trouble began, felt that he must *apologize* for his imminent reappearance, as something which she was unable to enjoy. 'I am so dreadfully sorry, my darling, that I have never been able to make you feel about me like Peggy feels about Geoff.'

Andrew and I, although no one we knew had been divorced, were aware of it as a possibility. From time to time we said to each other: 'Why don't they get divorced? It would be better than all this quarrelling.' It was years before it dawned on me that, given the law as it was then, if they had, we would have lost her. An aunt would presumably have been recruited to look after us: one of my father's two unmarried sisters, both of whom we liked well enough as aunts but who were unthinkable as mother-substitutes. Once I was grown-up, the thought of how much had been preserved for us by their decision to stay together made me profoundly grateful, though it was always painful to know of their pain.

It was institutionalized romanticism that did the damage: the fatal glorification of sexual excitement into Falling In Love, the dangerous concept of marriage as being In Love For Life. My mother had accepted those notions wholeheartedly, so when she found herself offending against them she thought herself nothing less than wicked. I am sure that she believed no one else among 'our sort of people' (people in books and so on didn't count) had ever done what she had done: a fearful burden to carry, but at that time unquestioned.

And even now I hesitate to say plainly what I myself believe about marital infidelity, because I know how cold-blooded it will seem to many people, among them some whom I love.

I believe that when the first flush of delight at being together has passed, infidelity is certainly not inevitable, but is and always has been very likely to take place if occasion offers. In most people's lives occasion offers only rarely unless pursued, and some people choose not to pursue, but not many will reject it if it turns up, as became perfectly clear during the war. I also believe that if infidelity does not cause heartbreak in a spouse or deprive children of a parent, and if it cheers up the two rule-breakers, thereby adding to the pleasure abroad in the world, it does no harm. I have never, therefore, seen any reason for all the mopping and mowing which goes on about it.

I do think, however, that even in the best-managed cases a couple ought to be very sure indeed that they understand each other before they indulge in mutual confession. For those who dislike dishonesty this is quite hard to accept – but think of what Tolstoy put poor Sonia through by his gross self-indulgence in honesty! It is up to the unfaithful to recognize the damage that might result from their conduct, and to avoid it if possible. Though of course they may, in their turn, start romanticizing what they are doing; and that, only too often, will cause mayhem. Falling In Love! I can still remember the ravishing sensation, the surge of vitality which gave brightness to the eyes and shine to the hair, the intoxication of it, as against the warm nourishing glow of plain *loving*. But 'intoxication' is what it is: it is as seductive and dangerous as alcohol, and should be handled as cautiously. How generations of romanticizing Romance can be counter-balanced is hard to see, but it ought to be done.

It is sad to think of my parents condemned to go through all their adult lives without any loving sex, harnessed together as mutual sources of unhappiness and guilt. It does, however, become less sad if I look at their marriage as a whole, because that reveals that they did somehow manage to develop the muscle to bear their burden. After he came home from Ethiopia it appears that both became less vulnerable, and when his job gave him the chance to live for six years in Southern Rhodesia (as Zimbabwe was then called), not only did she agree to accompany him, but she also enjoyed the experience. They had first to travel across Africa, sharing the driving of a truck, then build a house, living in a pair of *rondavels* until it was finished, and once he started managing the factory he had been sent to set up, she found much interest and entertainment in running their establishment and made many friends. They came back to England with a working companionship in place, and when he died in 1968, twenty years before she did, it was his generosity and gentleness that lived on in her mind. And she, in her long widowhood, was far from showing any sign of being embittered by past sadness. Instead she became calmer, kinder, wiser and more practically creative than most old women: someone who, rather than nurturing her sorrows, had preserved and worked on all the elements in her life – and there were many – that were worth having. Neither of them, in fact, allowed their less than happy marriage to become, in the end, as tragic as it might have been.

As children we, of course, had no idea of any reason why it might be tragic. All we knew was that there were rows, which we hated. I think Andrew knew more clearly than I did how much he hated them – he was younger than I was, and more vulnerable. I often managed to make myself think that I was irritated rather than frightened: 'How can they be *so silly*?' I used to say to myself; or, more often, 'How can *he* be so silly, always doing just the thing to make her lose her temper?' Because although it was clear to me that it was usually my mother who started the row, it was always my father I blamed for it. I 'sided' – we all three did, strongly – with her. Somehow – God knows how, because she certainly never *said* anything to indicate it – the fact that he had become repulsive to her conveyed itself to us, and as her nerves twanged, so did ours. What we desperately wanted when they were rowing was not that she would pull herself together and stop it, but that *he would go away*.

My grandmother was to say to me one day, when I was grown-up, 'Poor little girl, those quarrels used to make you so ill,' and I was astonished. Later still, when I had observed my own reactions to the stress of living in London during the bombing raids, I understood that she was right. I used to be surprised by the extent to which I was *not* frightened by the raids – but for the first time since I was a little girl I began to suffer again from colitis. So *that* was why I used to get those tummy-aches and sick-attacks when I was a child! I had been able to feel that I didn't so very much mind the rows because I *wasn't* minding them, I was stomaching them. And on consideration, I think I was lucky. It was a less painful way of getting through something bad than being fully aware of how bad it was, as my brother was.

But for us, quarrelling parents were not nearly – not anything like – so bad as they would have been if we had been less lucky in our circumstances. For one thing, there was always a buffer state of relations, nannies, governesses, housemaids, grooms, gardeners, farm friends around us, going on in its usual way, *continuing to be the same*, whatever was happening between our parents. It was one of those people who provided us with a useful formula: 'Your mummy and your daddy are both very nice people: it's just that perhaps they oughtn't to have got married to each other.' Andrew and I often used to repeat this formula and found it efficacious: it was the sort of thing grown-ups said, so it gave a feeling of detachment and superiority. And in addition to all these helpful people we had something even more valuable. We had space.

We came nearest to not having it when we lived for a couple of years in a five-bedroomed house in Hertfordshire with no land of its own except an orchard and a paddock. By then we had graduated from nursery to schoolroom, so we were eating all our meals with the grown-ups. Neither parent wished to shut us away (we were never shut away at any time, it was only that the layout of the larger house allowed much more spreading-out). So in 'the cottage' our family mingled closely all day except during lesson-time, and tensions had to be experienced by us all. Ursula's benign presence prevented it from being hell, but it was certainly a great deal worse than it ever was in Gran's house or the Farm, where we could simply disappear into our own world, forget the grown-ups, and enjoy life as much as ever. It chills my blood to think what it

must be like for the children – the many, many children – of
quarrelling parents who have to live without the space in which to
create a world of their own.

The other source of pain was our own behaviour, and the pain was
inflicted on the two cousins younger than ourselves.

Although we were the recipients of affectionate attention
from older cousins, we did not transmit it onwards. Even Patience,
before she became old enough to be a friend, received little from
Andrew and me but teasing and irritable tolerance. I have sometimes
watched with surprise and admiration the unselfconscious way
a group of working-class children will accept responsibility for a
baby, if their mother has sent it out in their care. If anyone had
suggested such a task to us we would have gone on strike. One
reason for this was, I think, the nursery/schoolroom split: when
you moved out of the nursery you began to live a life quite
different from that of the children still in it – even to see a good
deal less of them. But Joyce and Anne had continued to be kind to
us across that divide, so I fear that Andrew and I simply had less
generous natures. And he, after having felt the stress of our
parents' misery more acutely than I did, had then been forced to
endure intense unhappiness by being sent away, at the age of eight,
to boarding school: an unhappiness which naturally affected his
behaviour.

To be sent away from home was the most frightful thing either
of us could possibly imagine. I didn't have to imagine it until
much later, when I was old enough to understand the reasons
for it. Andrew knew that it was going to happen because it
happened to all boys, but at the age of eight there is a big gap
between the theoretical knowledge of something and the thing
itself. When they actually put him in a car, drove him off and
handed him over he had no alternative to bearing what felt
unbearable.

He has never said that he was bullied at school, and he was quite
a tough little boy so probably he wasn't. He was just exiled from all
that he most passionately loved, in a place where nothing spoke to

him. For a long time I kept two poems he sent me, one from his preparatory school, the other from Wellington, his public school: pathetic, clumsy little poems, one headed BURN THIS AT ONCE and the other NOT TO BE SHOWN TO ANYONE, 'anyone' underlined three times. Both were about being in a cold, dark place, dreaming of spring and birdsong and a dewy morning, then waking up and there, still, was the coldness and darkness.

*Andrew (with catapult) and John on the terrace*

So I knew he was unhappy. But I cannot remember thinking much about it – or feeling much about it, for that matter. Certainly I never questioned his fate: boys had to go to boarding schools, it was what always happened to them, poor things, and there was nothing anyone could do about it. Meanwhile I had my friendships with Pen and with other girls who did lessons with me, I had my ponies, I had my books, I had falling in love . . . I had moved out of the world I used to share with Andrew, when we busied ourselves together like squirrels or moles in the branches or the roots of adult life. The world I was now inhabiting was quite different. Only years later, when I was in my thirties, did I have a dream which told me how much I had known.

I dreamt that he and I, in high spirits, were running across grass together – and suddenly he was gone. I turned to see what had become of him and there were two men in uniform crouched over something stretched on the ground. Curious, and still happy, I ran back towards them, calling out 'What have you got there?' – and it was Andrew. One of the men half-rose and turned towards me, his eyes glaring; the other crouched lower over Andrew, one hand on his throat, the other clamped over his mouth. A scream of horror jolted out of me, waking me, and I lay there hearing my own voice moaning: 'Poor little boy – oh poor, poor little boy.'

It is easy to see how it worked on him. Having been exiled by the people he had thought to be his infallible protectors, when he was allowed back for limited periods he slid into rejecting them: an exile they had made him so an exile he would be. What had *not* rejected him was the place. He had been sent away from it, but it was still there, waiting for him. So what he did when he came back was burrow as deeply into the place, and stay as far from the family, as he could. It was not an instant or complete process, but gradually it became apparent that his preferred friends were boys from the village, his preferred dress was a smelly old many-pocketed gamekeeper's waistcoat, his preferred speech was broad Norfolk. At school he did as badly as he could (he would have to spend a year at a crammer before he could get into an agricultural college), and at home he behaved as badly as he dared. Which was sometimes so shamefully badly that it included tormenting a little boy eight years younger than himself.

Our two youngest cousins, Barbara and Colin, never felt as the rest of us did that they belonged to our beloved place. Barbara, with her brother Jimmy, had come for short visits when she was very young indeed, and had then been carried away to India by her parents; and in India the family was tragically stricken: Jimmy fell ill, and died. While we as little children had been wrapped snugly in the fabric of country life in Norfolk, she as a little child had been exposed to a blast of pain beyond our imagining. Her father's posting as Commander-in-Chief of a district centring on Bangalore still had two years to run, so her parents could not return at once to England. Feeling that they must not risk keeping Barbara and her little brother Colin in India, they first sent Colin and his nanny home to Gran's house, and about a year later her mother brought Barbara back too, and left her there. It would be for only a year, and where could the children be better cared for?

To a child of seven, 'only a year' might as well have been five or ten years; and my grandmother and her resident daughter, an aunt very dear to me, must have suffered some kind of blackout to their imaginations. They were not, of course, positively unkind, but to Barbara they did not seem loving. Perhaps no one could have seemed adequately loving, now that she was so far away from her very loving parents; but I do faintly remember comments about 'a rather sulky little girl' which suggest that they failed to understand how deeply unhappy she was – how traumatic Jimmy's death had been, and how it was possible for 'home' to be utterly unlike home to someone very young, lonely and unhappy, to whom it had never been anything of the sort.

When her parents came back they found a house in Dorset which worked a happy spell on Barbara and which she would later remember rather as we remembered Gran's house. But the latter had acquired unhappy associations. While she and Colin had been parentless there she had known not only loneliness, but anxiety: she had had to protect Colin – or so she felt – from Andrew. No doubt my brother would have protested 'I was only teasing him'; but teasing is always ambiguous and often masks cruelty (to which that protest can add a nasty little twist), and my sister confirms that at that time Andrew was often 'really horrid' to his juniors. I think that 'tormenting' was what the 'teasing' felt like to the victim and looked like to Barbara.

It was a shock to me when she told me about it, because I never had the least inkling of it. There were eight years between Barbara and me, and only two between me and Andrew, yet I had somehow contrived to ignore his unhappiness, and had been oblivious to the resulting 'horridness'. The picture it brings to my mind is of chickens pottering contentedly about their run as though nothing were wrong, while in a corner a group of them is pecking all the feathers out of one of their number.

My own theory about the boarding school phenomenon is that it was a reaction by the leisured classes to infantile sexuality. When a young Victorian mother (and my own mother was still Victorian in this respect) gazed fondly at her sweet, innocent baby boy in his nakedness, and suddenly his tiny penis stood up, I think she was horrified. Surely this little being, right at the start of life, couldn't have anything to do with what men liked to do in bed . . . but look at it! It clearly had. There, in the male creature, was the old Adam, even now.

So with boys you had to be very careful: however adorable they were, it was not wise to hug or kiss them too much. Some mothers even tried to turn them into girls, but that was obviously wrong – you wanted your little boy to grow up into a manly man, of course you did. But God forbid that the manliness should start before it had to, or that it should get out of hand. So the best thing to do was to isolate boys from the feminine, the sensuous, even before they could fully perceive it – to give them to trainers who would teach them to consume all their energy by *running about* a great deal . . .

It was not a problem that exercised the working classes, because their sons had to get out there and work as soon as they were out of short pants (or sooner – an old man in our village had been hired out to a farmer by his dad to pick stones off fields when he was eight years old). It arose from having time, as well as space. Of course boarding schools soon became muffled in blah about forming character and training boys to be leaders of men; and of course some families simply found it boring to have unfinished young people underfoot. But ours liked having us there, they wept genuine tears as they sent their little boys away. The imperative at work was a primitive one.

It is extraordinary that the men assented to it even more eagerly than the women. One can only assume that most men, being able to recognize their own sexiness, could easily, if caught young enough, be made to see it as bad; and then found it hard to understand the various kinds of damage done to them by this crude way of suppressing it. Or rather, of trying to suppress it, because naturally it did not succeed. My brother, for one, was to spend a good deal of his youth being far from seemly in his sexual behaviour.

But he did grow up to be a likeable man. He was to become the fond and understanding father of four sons, none of whom he sent to boarding school; and at Christmas lunch in his eightieth year he could look round the table at which sat all those sons, their wives and their children, and make the following pronouncement: 'At the risk of embarrassing you all horribly, and making my wife very cross, I want to say something. I want to say that *I have never been happier in all my life than I am today* when I look round this table and see you all here, still wanting to come back to us.' And when I said to him after lunch: 'And not only do they all still want to come back, but they're such an interesting lot, as well as being so nice,' he looked very sheepish and mumbled: 'I suppose you could say that Mary and I must have done *something* right' – which had, indeed, been evident for many years.

The truth is that although there are people who are permanently twisted out of shape as a result of painful childhood experiences, a great many more are not. And my brother is one of them.

# FALLING IN LOVE

FALLING IN LOVE resembled riding, in that it was always there, even before I was aware of it. I can remember being told that I had wanted to marry a boy called John Sherbroke, but not the wanting: all that remains of that boy is a moment of embarrassment when he had come to tea, and Nanny, about to lift him out of his high chair, asked him 'Do you want to sit down?' That was her euphemism for using the chamber-pot, and I knew at once from his puzzled expression that in the Sherbroke nursery it must be called something else. Sure enough, he said 'I *am* sitting down,' and Nanny was slightly flustered. She had been silly, I thought. She should just have offered him the pot. The first infatuation that I can remember is the one with Denis, the gardener's boy, which happened when I was about four – or so I believe for reasons given when I described the experience in *Stet*. It took the form of romantic daydreams.

The only daydream material provided by the world came from fairy stories: no newspapers or magazines crossed the threshold of the nursery (Mum's *Vogue* came later), there was no television, grown-ups didn't talk to us about love. It was from fairy stories that I formed my notion of what glamour was: a princess. The Sleeping Beauty, Cinderella, the many princesses who had to be competed for by princes and who were won by the sons of humble men, that tiresome princess who was kept awake by a pea under a huge pile of mattresses (it was not possible quite to believe in that one): all of them ensured that the companions of Hal and Thomas were princesses, and that it was a princess I was trying to turn into when I called on the magic of dressing-up. But when I fell in love I didn't dream of myself as a princess being courted: that was too far from reality. Instead I used a different scenario, and where I got it from I do not know . . . Or didn't, until I reached this very point, when suddenly a name was spoken in my head: Grace Darling.

Of course it was Grace Darling, the gallant daughter of the lighthouse keeper, rowing her boat through the raging waves to rescue the shipwrecked sailors. *She* came into the nursery: nannies and nursery-maids loved to tell her story, and in some nurseries (not ours, alas) to sing her song. Jessica Mitford wrote a book about Grace and her myth, and could still sing her song with great spirit when I last met her, not long before her death; but I had forgotten her for years and years, until I first heard Jessica mention her. And now I remember her again, because she it must have been who sent me up cliffs, down pits, into burning houses, across flooding rivers, to rescue imperilled Denis, or Wilfred the cowman's son.

Those were deeply satisfying daydreams, because after the excitement of the rescue came the finale, in which my beloved, recovering from his swoon, opened his eyes and saw me bending over him. At that point Grace Darling retired and a princess took over: *my* princess, the essential me, the one Pen was not allowed to play. The princess with the cloud of night-black hair.

By the time David, recognized by me as my first real love and even acknowledged as such by other people, came on the scene, both Grace and the princess were beginning to fade out. I was eight when his parents rented the Hall Farm for a year: *our* house, because we had lived in it for a while when Dad was abroad (and would return to it when he was working in London). We were staying with Gran when this family of strangers moved in, and Andrew and I, all set for hostilities, crossed the back park and the water meadow on a scouting expedition, to size the invaders up.

David was away at school. It was his younger brother Robin

whom we met in the orchard, a small stout figure in a blue coat who turned his back on us to stomp away through the apple trees – shy rather than inimical, as it turned out. We followed him at a distance. When he climbed into one of the very old, half-fallen-down trees, we climbed after him. Whereupon something about him decided us almost at once that he was not a pubby, so we stopped resenting him and he became a friend.

Robin often referred to his big brother in a way which suggested that when David came home for the holidays we should respect him. He could do things we couldn't do, knew things we didn't know. Sometimes it was implied that if we got uppish David would put us in our place, which might have made us wary of him, but didn't. Robin was so much our kind of person that we were happy to fall in with his attitude, and looked forward eagerly to his brother's homecoming.

I don't remember *falling*, only *having fallen*: the hollow shape of love was in existence before we met, and was then gradually filled with this new reality. What I am sure of is that of all the loves in my life this was the most soundly based. I loved him because he was kind, brave, honest and reliable: a boy gentle to those younger than himself, who never seemed tempted to show off and who could check a dangerous game, such as climbing the hay-elevator with its rows of sharp up-curving prongs, without fearing that anyone would think him sissy.

When we were together, as we often were, in a group of my cousins and his, we were friends. Loving him made me happy if he picked me when choosing a team for a game, and even happier if he danced with me at a party, though he didn't dance very well; but it did not clutter me with self-consciousness. I did not expect him to know that I loved him, nor did I mind his not knowing. We wrote to each other when he was away at school and I kept his letters tied up with a blue ribbon, going to bed delighted if one of them began 'My dear Di' instead of plain 'Dear Di', or ended 'Much love' instead of 'Love'. I daydreamed about him as I had about the others, but the dreams were less far-fetched.

The princess vanished for ever when I was eleven, meeting her end in the bathroom of the Hertfordshire house – an apt setting. There was, of course, only one bathroom in that house, and it was of the utmost austerity. I would be approaching my thirties before I knew anyone who made their bathroom pretty, and was older still before the words 'en suite' began to appear in the vocabulary of house agents. In that same dreary little bathroom my mother had recently told me about menstruation, saying that it was a terrible bore but that one got used to it and it didn't hurt – for which sensible approach I became grateful when a friend told me that *her* mother tried to make her call it 'my little friend'. I had started to let my hair grow, hoping for plaits long enough to sit on, and was disappointed because they refused to do more than touch my shoulders. Having wiped the steam from the mirror, I was leaning on the washbasin to study their progress when a chilling thought swam into my mind: however much my appearance changed when I grew up – and surely it would change quite a lot? – it *must*! . . . but however much it did, I was never going to have huge dark eyes and a cloud of black hair.

Never.

It was not possible.

Blue eyes and mouse-coloured hair that refused to be more than shoulder-length: that was me, so I had better lump it.

It was a hard thought to take. And from that day on, if I tried to push a daydream too far into fantasy it stopped working.

Sometimes I managed to persuade a daydream to climax in a kiss, but in real life the only time David and I made physical contact, beyond hauling each other up a wall or dancing, was when we were at an agricultural show with our parents and had wandered off together. We were enjoying the smell of trodden grass, the music of the brass band, the splendour of the Shire horses with their manes and tails so elaborately braided and cockaded with colour, the brooding serenity of the beef cattle, the gleaming vermilion and sky-blue paint on the wagons and tractors. We were having a good time together . . . and suddenly I realized with a jolt that we were arm in arm.

It was the most wonderfully disturbing thing that had ever

happened: too much to bear. As though the jolt had been an electric shock, we started apart. I blushed too violently to be able to look at him and see if he was blushing too. I raged at myself inwardly for my lack of control: why, oh why hadn't I hidden my noticing so that my arm could have stayed in his, and me aware of it? How long had we been walking like that? Perhaps for a long time, and *I had missed it*! And which of us had first reached for the other? I wanted desperately for it to have been he, but it was no good: nothing could be fetched up but that we had been close and at ease. And now we were behaving like grown-ups, sparing each other embarrassment by pretending nothing had happened. I loved him the more for the way he did this . . . but oh God, suppose it was I who had taken his arm and he had thought 'How silly' but had been too kind to make a sign . . . But if that had been so, surely he would not have been walking and talking so naturally at the moment when I noticed: even if I *did* make the first move he couldn't have minded. I was to treasure that afternoon for a long time.

But there were temptations to infidelity even during that first love. He was not a very articulate boy, and what he laughed at most readily was farce. He would thoroughly enjoy it if someone sat down where there wasn't a chair – indeed, amusing events of a banana-skin type made landmarks for him: 'the time the wasp got into Uncle Harry's shirt', 'the time Mummy put salt instead of sugar into the fruit salad': he would refer to such occasions with almost pious regularity. There came a time when boys who found humour in ideas rather than predicaments began to have charm for me.

The first of these tempted me badly. Tim. He gave an impression of recklessness as well as of wit, he had a gift for words, and grown-up ways which seemed almost awe-inspiringly sophisticated, and he lent much sparkle to our activities. It was he who dubbed dam-building 'dearie-me building' after we had been scolded for swearing. I repeated his witticisms constantly; I only had to say 'We built a dearie-me' to myself in order to giggle. I thought about him often, and saw the possibility of changing allegiance.

By then I must have been twelve, the boys in their early teens. A group of parents – ours, some of our cousins', and those of both boys – had decided to spend part of the summer holidays together in Devonshire, some of them camping, some in a nearby hotel. We were among the campers, organized with military precision by my father in a group of tents clustered round a marquee, two rough fields away from the top of high cliffs. It was a lovely place, across the estuary from Salcombe, to which we were rowed by a ferryman when we went shopping for supplies. Golden, shell-strewn sand in little cliff-bound coves, rock-pools full of limpets and sea anemones, and sparkling blue water – all this was astonishing to us, accustomed as we were to the austere seaside places of East Anglia where the most majestic sight would be – if you were lucky – a stretch of sand-dunes, and the sea washing the shingle was usually nearer to gravy-coloured than blue. The holiday must have been hard work for parents, but for us it was the best we had ever had, and for me it was extra-good because of love. Which boat would I go out in today, David's, or Tim's? Had either of them noticed my successful dive from the high rock? Which of them would come with me to the spring to fill the drinking-water bucket? It didn't really matter which, because the presence of either was enough to fill an occasion with pleasure; but although neither boy was aware of me as anything but one among several playmates, I felt that I ought to make a choice. It would be a private matter, entailing no change in conduct, but to me it seemed necessary.

But it did not seem simple. I had been loving David for what seemed to me as good as ever, and now that I saw the possibility of loving someone else I was shocked as well as thrilled. I had not known that I was capable of such fickleness.

One evening when the flaps of my tent had been hitched back because of the heat, I lay in my sleeping bag doing two things at once: watching night fall, and reaching a decision. How could I be comfortable in my skin if I didn't know who I loved? Nightfall was beautiful and decision-making was important. Again and again my eyes followed the line of a distant, heathery hill, which swept down and then slightly up again to end in a promontory jutting out to sea. I wanted to fix its profile in my mind (I was always storing up nostalgia), and the way its colours slowly blurred into the darkness of a silhouette, and the sky's cool green deepened to night-colour. And I wanted to catch a star at the moment of its becoming visible, which seemed to be impossible. I stared at an empty piece of sky, glanced away for a moment, looked back – and there was a star as though it had always been present. The air was moist on the exposed part of my face, so I knew the grass was already thick with dew, and a cricket was chirruping, though not under my groundsheet as sometimes happened. Going to sleep out of doors in this wild place was so beautiful that it gave me an ache in my heart. And which of the two boys did I love?

David, of course. Alas. I felt cool inside, and solid, as though I had dug down to a base of some sort. 'What a pity', I thought, because I would so much have enjoyed loving Tim. But it wasn't David's fault that he was less amusing. It would be disloyal to abandon him because of that, when he had been a part of my life for so long. And he was so kind, so generous, so good – how could I turn against someone who had done nothing but continue to be himself? When I thought of him, his rival's very charm seemed a source of unfair advantage of which I could not approve. David was to remain my love for another two years, until I met the man, in my eyes grown-up, to whom I would eventually become engaged.

There was no – or no conscious – physicality in these early loves, yet while they were going on I was spending a great deal of time thinking about sex. Indeed, from the age of eleven, when revelation occurred, except when my mind was being positively invaded in one way or another, I thought of little else.

Revelation took the form of a small black book with nothing written on its cover. Why I pulled it out of a bookcase's bottom shelf where it was tucked away in a corner, I cannot imagine, but when I had read on its title-page the words 'Wise Parenthood' I started to turn the pages, supposing I was about to discover some method of raising children properly that my mother had once hoped to follow. As a result, I was never to suffer what she suffered on her honeymoon. From that early age I knew – not approximately but exactly – what men and women do in bed; and I also knew that it was one of life's best pleasures, and that I was going to start enjoying it *the minute I was old enough*.

The revelatrix was Marie Stopes, that absurd – even monstrous – woman who yet did more for her fellow-women than almost anyone else in the twentieth century. She made contraception acceptable, and on the way there she taught everyone who read her what she taught me. And in my case her lessons were supplemented by a posse of bawdy balladeers who had been collected into six volumes bound in white leather which dwelt in my grandfather's smoking room. Those, too, I fell on by chance.

Every year, either just before or just after the great Spring Cleaning to which her house was always subjected under Hannah's generalship, Gran 'did' Gramps's books. His library was extensive and valuable, in her eyes almost sacred, so that no one else was allowed to clean the books, not even Hannah. Gran would put on a cotton overall and one of her sunbonnets to keep the dust out of her beautiful white hair, and every single book she would take out, clap-clap to blow away any dirt settling between the pages, wipe with a soft clean duster, and (if the binding was leather) polish with a special unguent which she kept in a stone jar. She did the library, the morning room and the smoking room, and it took her weeks.

She was halfway through the smoking room when I went in to loll on the sofa and keep her company. The handsome white volumes, which she had piled on the floor near the desk, caught my eye, and I saw the word 'Ballads' on their spines. 'What are those?' I asked, with what I thought was virtuous curiosity – ballads were supposed to appeal to children because they were usually hearty, but they bored me. 'You wouldn't be interested in those,' said Gran, much too quickly – and in a flash my secret prowler was on to it. That evening, as soon as the house's silence assured me that the grown-ups were safely in the drawing room or the servants' hall, I nipped down and abducted one of the volumes to read under my bedclothes. In those days we didn't use the expression 'Wow' – but 'WOW' it was.

So I was unusually well-informed for my age, and I found the information wildly exciting – and yet, being in love was one of the things that served to take my mind off sex. I find it surprising now, but *then* it didn't enter my head that it should be otherwise. Children – because the word 'teenagers' was not yet in use, 'children' included people a good deal older than it includes now – children did not *do* sex. If a child of thirteen or fourteen dressed or behaved in contradiction of this 'fact', I saw them much as I saw someone who dressed or behaved in the wrong way when riding to hounds: absurd, and lacking in taste. When, in my mid-teens, I learnt that someone I actually knew had in fact 'done it', I was appalled – so much so that for a day or two I believed I would never recover from the shock; which was an odd reaction considering that what had been done was something I myself had been dreaming of eagerly for – by then – at least five years. (Fortunately my recovery from this shock was very much more rapid than I expected it to be.)

Women much younger than I am, belonging to generations in which lovemaking between teenagers is taken for granted, sometimes say that they embarked on sex when they did chiefly because it was expected of them: they would have looked silly to their contemporaries if they had been unwilling. Which makes me suppose that my own lack of resentment at having to wait so long to be 'old enough' was largely due to there being no peer pressure. If everybody you know, young as well as old, is thinking in the same way, you need to be a strongly dissident person to think differently. And it is possible – even probable – that some part of me was glad to be given so much time.

The acceptance of a constraint which may seem strange to many people nowadays, gained me, in the years between fourteen and eighteen, an intense experience of erotic pleasure, getting nearer and nearer to that of full lovemaking, which was thoroughly enjoyable. The first time a man's hand closed on mine and I turned mine so that our palms met was so exquisitely exciting that it still stirs me to remember it. Then came the first time someone sitting beside me in the back of a car put an arm round me and pulled me towards him so that my head rested on his shoulder; the first time a man, having done that, brushed my forehead with his lips (urgent question: would it be cheating to count that as *being kissed*?); the first real kiss, followed by the first open-mouthed kiss; the first hand on a breast, followed by the first unbuttoning leading to hand and lips on a bare breast (a tremendously exciting leap forward, that was) . . . And so it went on, incident by incident, each one pondered, savoured, dreamt about: the haze of sexy daydreaming through which I floated in those days must have been almost tangible.

It didn't matter much who was doing the touching or kissing, because I had fallen in love when I was fifteen (goodbye, dear David, goodbye!) and was quite sure that it was Paul's bed into which I would eventually sink; but he was five years older than I was and I had to catch up with him before I could expect him to fall in love with me. I was practising . . . and loving every moment of it.

Dances were where it mostly happened, ranging from modest 'hops' in small houses to full-scale balls in big ones, and including going with a group of friends to places such as the Assembly Rooms in Norwich where public dances were held, usually on a Saturday night. Mine was the first generation of country-house girls allowed to go to dances unchaperoned. To begin with we were driven in my grandmother's sedate car (complete with fur rug, footwarmer and speaking-tube) by Mr Youngman, her chauffeur, who collected us at midnight. The earliest moves in love's game were therefore given an extra thrill by taking place secretly, under that rug. But soon young men with wheels were invited to dinner and drove us to the dances . . . The true beginning of the sexual revolution for us came long before the sixties, with the car. Once a man and girl who had been dancing together all evening were able to drive home alone together in that little capsule of safe privacy, the deliciously slow progress towards loss of virginity accelerated to a rush.

Being sent to boarding school helped to check this rush, as far as I was concerned, and probably for other girls, too (though I gained the impression that I was looking forward to its conclusion more eagerly than most of my friends). School happened to me when I was fourteen, and made freedom part-time. A result of no one's recognizing the teens as a separate condition was impatience to be grown-up: although I no longer felt like a child, I was having to bide my time before bursting forth as what I did feel like, which was more or less adult. Boarding school was a good way of getting through this not-quite-yet time; it controlled restlessness within a discipline that I could accept because it was part of the set-up as a whole, not directed at me as an individual.

There was one moment, some time in my seventeenth year, when I broke ranks. A particularly good dance was being given by some grand neighbours of ours, not long before the end of my school's winter term. It seemed a pity that I should miss it, so much so that my mother hit on a solution: my teeth did in fact need attention, so she asked my headmistress if she could take me for a day's visit to a London dentist, which would mean keeping me out for a night – and the date of the dentist's appointment (this, of course, was not revealed) was that of the dance, for which we could get back from London just in time. It was a delightfully daring plan: no present-day schoolgirl can have any idea of the convent-like seclusion imposed by headmistresses in my day. Letters were censored, outings apart from those at half-term were forbidden, no girl was ever allowed to leave the school grounds alone, and it didn't occur to anyone that parent and child might communicate by telephone. Permission to visit a London dentist was a favour so great that even by its agonizing self (no injections in those days except for extractions) it would have been a treat.

Early on the morning after the dance my father drove me back to school, and left a note for the headmistress, with whom he got on well, confessing that I had been to a dance. His almost obsessive honesty compelled him to it, but he certainly didn't feel that he was purging a serious sin: he expected her to find it funny.

Instead, I was summoned to her study and threatened with expulsion. So violently did she berate me that what began as a schoolgirl's dismay at being found out suddenly switched to an adult's astonishment at absurd over-reaction, so that when at last she thundered: 'Have you no sense of honour at all?' I answered coldly: '*Not* if that is what you mean by a sense of honour.' I can no longer remember how the interview ended, except for having a gratifying sense that she was disconcerted; and she must, when she recovered from her rage, have seen that she was making a mountain out of a molehill. She did, to my father's amusement, write him a pompous little note telling him that he had not behaved like a gentleman, but she did not expel me – indeed, I ended as the school's head girl. The incident remained in my mind as a pleasing one – the tip of a toe in the sea of being grown-up.

At no time was school as painful for me as it had been for Andrew. A person of fourteen has a better sense of time than one of eight, so although the thirteen weeks of my first term looked hideously long, they did not look endless, and even during that term I could see the point of being educated. Later, although my recognition of the school's quality was always grudging and I never stopped wanting to be free of it, I did see that as schools went it was a good one. I enjoyed the friends I made there, it taught me a lot and got me into Oxford, and it also turned me round and shoved me gently but firmly away from what was behind me, towards real life.

*Diana Athill, 2000*

# NOW

L OOKING BACK, I see that I moved away from childhood expecting the answer 'Yes!' And to begin with it *was* a return to Eden – to the house, the horses, the dances, the freedom to read what I liked – and an Eden with wider horizons than formerly. There was a year between school and university which I spent at home as a grown-up, which might have become claustrophobic if I had thought it would last longer than that, but Oxford was coming and after Oxford real life, so I felt free to luxuriate in that year rather than to chafe at its restrictions.

It is extraordinary that in 1935–36 anyone could have felt so sure that the future was going to be happy. At school we had access to all the serious newspapers and weeklies, and were encouraged to think about what we read. Considering myself a serious-minded girl, I had also read a certain amount of left-wing and pacifist literature: I knew that Britain was a scandalous mess and that the Versailles Treaty had sown the seeds of a second world war, and I had responded by glibly declaring myself a socialist and a pacifist. But my guts were not listening to my head.

I was not alone in this. The Sunday *Observer*, more than any other newspaper, was alert to what was going on in Germany and prescient as to where it was heading: every weekend its Cassandra-like leaders wailed their warning. And my father cancelled his subscription. This was not because he disbelieved the message, but because he found it all too easy to believe. He knew what he was going to do when the worst happened: he was on the reserve, so he would be back in the Army straight away without a moment's hesitation; but he was damned if he was going to waste good time brooding on it in advance. And I suppose I, in a less reasoned way, felt the same. But how I managed to make this work – to go on actually *feeling* as though my future was a happy one – I can't explain.

Perhaps it was being in love, and knowing at last that the man I called Paul in *Instead of a Letter*, for whose response I had been waiting trustfully since I was fifteen, was now in love with me. We were going to be married (he was in the RAF, flying bombers: why was I not terrified for him?). So perhaps the gut-expectation of the answer 'Yes!' came from my certainty of that, as much as it did from conditioning. I ought to have been able to feel the reality of the 'No!' which was soon to come to the world's peace, but I had no way of foreseeing the 'No!' ahead of me within my own life.

Both came. The gates of Eden clanged shut. I have told the story of unhappy love and my recovery from it in *Instead of a Letter*, so I will say no more here than that first his letters stopped coming, then one came asking me to release him from our engagement because he was about to marry someone else, and soon after that he was killed. I have also, in *Stet*, told the story of the good life I had in publishing in spite of this unhappiness – some of it even while the unhappiness was still there. And now I can see more clearly than I used to, how the roots of this life-saving career can be traced back to the childhood I have been describing in this book.

Someone from a family in which everyone obviously found books one of life's main sources of pleasure could hardly fail to grab at a chance to work in publishing if offered. I had been brought up in the knowledge that books were fun, as well as important. My father's passion for P. G. Wodehouse, which I shared, almost amounted to an addiction, so that when he came home with the latest Wodehouse which he, naturally, had to finish before anyone else could so much as touch it, I was so frantic at having to wait for it that I would have darted in and snatched it if he had given me the smallest chance. And at the same time the greatness of great writers was seen as greatness of the most solemn kind. Books were up there with nature and love as the things which mattered most.

And so, in my old age, they still are. To me the radio always meant music, so when my hearing began to go I listened less and less, and now not at all; and television, which never seemed as enjoyable as I hoped it would be, has become something for which I can rarely be bothered to walk into the next room (I wouldn't dream of having it in my own). So books are impossible to do without.

Some of this dependence is a matter of habit: lacking a book which I actually want to read, I will munch away on one which means little to me, though never on one which annoys me – I would rather clean the silver or patch a sheet than do that. And when this happens, I will forget the book within a week. Most often it will be a novel because fiction, these days, has to be more than just well-written (as most of it is) to hold me. Like most of the old people I know, what I am looking for is material for my own imagination to work on, rather than experience predigested by someone else into a story.

The fiction-writers I am still able fully to enjoy are those like Alice Munro, Raymond Carver, Pat Barker or Hilary Mantel who pay such close attention to their subject that one almost forgets their intervention between oneself and whatever it is. 'Look-at-me!' writing of the Martin Amis kind, much as it attracts many people, has always left me cold, as do fanciful capers however inventive. To me they seem to intrude between the reader and the raw material of life, rather than to illuminate it, and never having had much patience with them, now I have none. Although eccentricity does not necessarily put me off. A recent discovery, David Foster Wallace, who seems to be obsessional almost to the point of madness so that too often he threatens to smother the reader, has nevertheless done some of the best writing I have ever read, for which I am very grateful.

As well as turning more often to non-fiction, I indulge in

another habit common among old people: rereading old favourites, some of them so old as to come from my earliest days. In the little Norfolk house where I spend many weekends there are shelves still full of books from my cousin's childhood, many of which also figured in mine, and it is amusing to pull out, say, *The Count of Monte Cristo* and find that it is, indeed, an excellent story; or one of Daphne du Maurier's lesser works and think 'Oh my God, how could I *ever* . . . !' A few books which I read greedily, not in childhood but as a very young woman, I avoid reading again because I suspect they would fill me with shame: the novels of Charles Morgan, for instance, best sellers in their day, well reviewed and eagerly consumed by many, including me – and now I'm pretty sure they were pretentious garbage. And some of my most beloved books – those of Tolstoy and Jane Austen, for example – I have deliberately left aside for a long time because I want to come back to them once more before I die with a fresh eye.

Two other occupations which I love, and which came to me late in life as though they were discoveries, grew in fact from long-buried roots: gardening and needlework.

My mother and my aunts were enthusiastic and knowledgeable gardeners and I always enjoyed what their enthusiasm produced, but I never felt the smallest tingle of interest in the actual occupation of gardening – never pulled a weed or sowed a seed, or imagined myself doing so in the future, until I was in my sixties, when Barbara, leaving London to do a six-year stint for her paper in Washington, said to me rather apologetically: 'Do you think you could just sort of keep an eye on the garden so that it doesn't go *quite* wild?' The garden was a neglected London lawn with a rose-bed at one side of it, full of valiant roses which had been old when we moved into the house. It had one crab-apple tree planted when Barbara's son was born, a vast laurel and even vaster and fiendishly thorny pyracantha which combined to shade most of the space, and very little charm. It had served a happy purpose as a playground for children and habitat for guinea-pigs, but had never been much loved for itself. The day after Barbara left I leant out of my bedroom window, gave the garden a long look, and found myself thinking 'There's nothing for it: I'll have to re-seed the lawn and do the whole thing over from scratch'. Which I did, at considerable expense of money and work, and as soon as one plant put into the earth by my own inexpert hands performed the miracle of actually *growing*, I was hooked.

Now, alas, I can no longer do more than a very little gardening with my own hands, and have had greatly to simplify the London garden; but in the much larger and more complicated Norfolk garden I have luckily been able to call on the help of a neighbour who is as full of ideas as she is of energy, and – as we tell each other constantly – 'we are getting there'. And pottering about in it, doing the small things that I am still able to do, is a deep and peaceful pleasure.

That I also followed my mother into doing needlepoint embroidery is even odder, because I used to watch her at it with amazement – almost with horror – at the slowness of it, at the patience it required. If she decided that something had gone wrong, so that she must unpick what she had done and start again . . . no, I couldn't see how anyone could *bear* such a task, and as for finding it enjoyable . . . ! What tempted me into it was a book we published – *A Pageant of Pattern for Needlepoint Canvas* by a brilliant American amateur called Sherlee Lantz – which showed me that I could work to my own designs instead of following patterns painted on the canvas, as my mother had always done. Stitching your own design is far more exciting, because you are never quite sure how it's going to turn out. I had always wanted to paint and had even gone through a spell as a Sunday painter, abandoned when I realized that I was not going to be able to give enough time to it to become any good. Now I discovered that if I didn't think of myself as 'drawing', but simply as marking out what I wanted to put on the canvas – then I could in fact draw! And away I went, having a lovely time and not hesitating for a minute if it became apparent that something needed to be unpicked and done over again. It is true that there comes a time when one can't think of anyone else for whom to make a cushion or a chair-seat or a fire-screen or a hanging . . . but all the same, I expect I shall go back to it when I have finished writing. There is something astonishingly satisfying about holding in your hands a physical object that didn't exist until you made it.

If you took a group of octogenarians – let's say a hundred old reservoirs of experience – my guess is that about a quarter of them would *look* as though their contents were mostly disagreeable: as though, if they were turned inside out, you would see disappointment, disapproval, pain. None of my family has looked like that, and neither do I. And my reluctant conclusion is that this is because of the privileges we all enjoyed as a result of being born into the upper reaches of the middle class, and in the country.

To take the simplest things first: we were fed on ample amounts of healthy food, all of it fresh, and we had access to up-to-date medical care and sanitation and were taught the basic rules of hygiene such as enough sleep, plenty of fresh air and exercise, and don't drink too much. On top of that we were given good educations so that we could keep our minds occupied and find interest in a wide range of subjects, and enough leisure to indulge in enjoyable hobbies. And the standards of behaviour set by our forebears were reasonable, because they had not been *over*-privileged to the point of becoming arrogant or self-indulgent (that balance, I believe, has been important). In my generation, anyway, our childhood was directed with common sense as well as with love, and our surroundings were so secure and pleasant that we could be free of constant surveillance. And above all we lived in a place which we felt was ours and which we loved: we were rooted.

Of course I don't mean that people with other backgrounds cannot flourish. It is self-evident that they do – and remarkably, so do some people with backgrounds insalubrious enough to cripple, proof that innate qualities can withstand lack of nurture in a marvellous way. Those are the people who most deserve celebration: the ones who challenge easy pessimism about humanity, and who have warmed me, when I have met them, with currents of hope. Two of them, Morris Stock and Daphne Anderson, I remembered in *Stet*; and a third, to my great good fortune has become a friend in my old age: Andrea Ashworth, whose *Once in a House on Fire* never fails to leave a sort of amazed happiness in those who read it. The opposite can also be true: people born in fortunate circumstances can prove to have natures which warp in spite of it. So it would be absurd to claim too much on the grounds of any individual's experience, and all I mean to say is that it seems likely to be *easier* to reach a contented and sturdy old age if you have had my kind of luck, and I can't imagine myself having done so without it. Apart from anything else, there is that ingrained self-confidence which comes from the indecent sense of superiority which we were allowed to have as children. My own surface self-confidence was smashed when Paul jilted me, and I am not sure that I would have survived without the support of the secret – the inadmissible – self-confidence which underlay it.

But chiefly it is the place for which I am grateful, not as it now is, but as it was. It is that which constantly makes its way to the top of the rag-bag of memories that I have become. Suddenly I will see the chaffinch's nest which Pen and I found on a winter's morning when, under a hard blue sky, every single twig and thread was coated with sparkling hoarfrost. Chaffinches make the neatest, prettiest nest of all, and that one had been turned into an exquisite miracle of silver and diamonds. Or the stream above the weir which marks the lake's beginning, where it runs shallow under alders and we had decided to bathe naked – it seemed like a wild thing to do. We rode out to it bareback in nothing but cotton frocks, turned the ponies loose to graze, scrambled down the bank, stripped off our frocks – and found that the water didn't even reach our knees. Having got so far we felt we had to lie down in it, which was cold and uncomfortable because the bottom was gravel, not mud, which was why the water running limpid over gold had looked so tempting. And no sooner had we pulled on our frocks and vaulted onto our ponies (bare pony under wet bare bottoms felt very odd) than Aunt Joyce appeared, walking her dog. Why, she asked, were we wet? So we had to tell her – would she think our nakedness wicked? But when she said it would have made more sense to choose a deeper place and wear swimsuits she was laughing, so that was all right. Or the huge old hollow oak at the bottom of the farm orchard, with flames roaring out of it as though it was a giant's torch, when Andrew, then seven, had thought he could smoke out a wasps' nest (or was it a hornets'?) by lighting a fire inside it – the tree went on burning all night. Or the two trees in the orchard which bore little yellow apples, delicious if eaten off the branch but useless otherwise, on the day when my mother and I took our watercolour boxes and sat down to paint them in blossom – oh, the smell of apple-blossom on a sunny day! . . .

Here I am almost at my end, and my beginning rises up to meet me – or rather, even when I thought I was far away from it, it was always there, and now I have come back to it. And because in my eyes it was always so beautiful, it delights me yet again. It is too much to ask – I ought not to allow myself even to think of it – but perhaps it is not entirely impossible that I might, like my mother, come to the end of my days murmuring about some random memory: 'It was absolutely divine'.

*In the kitchen garden with Andrew, circa 1925*

# INSTEAD OF
# A LETTER

# Introduction

I FIRST MET Diana Athill when we shared a stage at a book
festival in the summer of 2000. We had come to Hay-on-Wye to
talk about the memoirs we had written: *Once in a House on Fire*,
about my growing up under tough circumstances in Manchester;
and *Stet*, about Athill's fifty years in London book publishing. At
eighty-two, this solidly confident and brisk lady was more than half
a century older than me. The audience might have imagined that,
other than our both having written about our lives, we had very
little in common. But we hit it off immediately. Surprisingly
youthful, Diana was formidable yet full of fun – and unafraid to talk
about things that others might shy away from. On that first
occasion, my pleasure in meeting her was heightened by an odd
sort of déjà vu, for in her voice and her eyes I recognized all the
humour and wisdom that I knew from her writing.

Athill's language combines immediacy, ease and precision of
expression. A lifetime of reading and editing makes itself felt in the
fine structure and pace of each of her books. Above all, she is a
virtuoso at what she calls 'seeing things'. Sitting down to write her
first story, she told herself, 'I'm going to get it *just as it was*.'

'My aunt and my own temperament equipped me with eyes,'
Athill says in *Instead of a Letter*, as she describes an enlightening
moment. 'I was drawing horses, as I constantly did, when [my
aunt] leant over my shoulder and said, "Draw a naked man – a man
or a woman."' The young Diana drew 'a shapeless forked radish'.
Seeing the look on her aunt's face, she knew 'that I had failed in

some way: that there was something of significance I should have been able to do with the human body instead of being embarrassed by it.'

That childhood epiphany occurred in the early 1920s; eighty years on, Diana Athill is recognized as a remarkably honest anatomist of human psychology. Her books bristle with intimacy. She looks at life, and herself, with peeling lucidity. Her writing is vivacious and unsentimental; often funny and painful in the same wince; piercing yet charming. These qualities shine through both her fiction and her non-fiction. Yet for most of her working life – spent as chief editor at the publishing house of André Deutsch, which she helped to found – Diana Athill did not regard herself primarily as a writer. She was forty-four years old when her first book, *Instead of a Letter*, was published in 1962. The autobiography of an ordinary person, someone of no great public eminence, *Instead of a Letter* was a curious work of non-fiction – what its author referred to as a 'documentary', and what we would today call a 'memoir'. Athill went on to publish several other books: a collection of short stories (*An Unavoidable Delay*, 1962), a novel (*Don't Look at Me Like That*, 1967) and two more 'documentaries' (*After a Funeral*, 1986 and *Make Believe*, 1993). But she never relinquished her day job, which offered her security and standing (she was known to be one of the best book editors in London) as well as satisfaction. As her work saved her from having to write for a living, she wrote only when she felt confident that she had something to say.

Athill's fifty years in publishing are the subject of her sixth book, *Stet*, which received enthusiastic and widespread acclaim in Britain (where it was published by Granta Books in 2000) and in North America. She had not published a book for almost a decade, and many readers were new to her lively and intelligent voice. *Stet* told the story of her relationship with André Deutsch (who died the year the book came out), the man who had been her boss, close friend and (briefly) lover, and narrated the history of the books she helped shape, giving sharp and entertaining cameos of authors such as V. S. Naipaul, Jean Rhys and Brian Moore. Memoirs set in the world of publishing make up a small and not particularly popular genre, but *Stet* broke out of the boundaries of its obvious audience (not a large one) and became, as many reviewers noted, that thing called a 'classic' – a book to be enjoyed by people who had never crossed a publisher's doorstep, had never wanted to, and never would. This was a victory for her skill as a writer, and for the personality in her writing. For all its candour and nuance, however, *Stet* is only obliquely self-revealing. Having introduced us to an individual already formed, it leaves us wondering how Athill came to be the person she is, how she came to see the way she sees.

*Instead of a Letter*, Athill's most personal book, allows us to watch the formation of that character. At its heart lies the tragic story of how she fell in love for the first time, eventually to suffer severe disappointment and attacks of grief and loneliness that eroded her self-esteem. In this memoir, we witness a soul first being drained of vitality, then slowly, painstakingly returning to life. We see Athill emerge, not only alive, but full of vivacity, blessed with a way of seeing that is lyrically sensitive yet grounded in a thumpingly pragmatic, sensibly-proportioned approach to herself and to life.

Athill's vision is especially remarkable given the insularity of her privileged background. 'There I used to be,' she writes of her idyllic beginnings in the Norfolk countryside, 'as snug and as smug as anyone, believing with the best that we were the best.' Born in 1917, the daughter of an army colonel, she spent much of her childhood at her grandparents' house where, in spite of her family's ailing finances,

necessities included a head gardener with two men under him, two grooms, a chauffeur, a butler and a footman, a cook and a kitchenmaid with a scullery maid to help them, a head housemaid with two under-housemaids, and my grandmother's lady's maid. They included, too, animals for our pleasure and governesses and schools for our instruction. They included books and a great deal of wholesome food, linen sheets rather than cotton, and three separate rooms for being in at different times of the day, not counting the dining-room, the smoking-room, the front hall, in which, for some reason, my grandmother always had tea, and the nursery.

Swathed in comfort, boasting an armigerous ancestry rich with 'rustic Athill knights', she seemed poised to grow up and go out into the world with her 'sense of superiority' unruffled. Yet, even at the age of ten, Diana had shocked her grandmother with a flight of fancy that suggested she understood there was a more turbulent world beyond the shelter of nursery teas:

> I thought that it was as though people were confined in a bowl which was floating on a sea. While snug at the bottom of the bowl they lived their lives complacently, but the bowl spun and tossed on the sea and its spinning sometimes sent one of them up its side until he could see over its rim. All round would be the endless chaos of dangerous, cold grey water, unsuspected till then, and anyone who had seen it and had understood that what he had thought was safety was only a little bowl, would not be able to bear it.

Through reading books and with the encouragement of the aunt who had nudged her to try her hand at drawing nudes, Diana began to sense that 'the family's way of thinking' was narrowly trammelled. Still, she galloped – largely unquestioning – through an adolescence that revolved around 'horses and sex', in which 'hours – weeks, months, years' were spent thinking about clothes. By the time she left school, she had grown to be an 'exuberant, slightly gauche girl', 'affected and a little arrogant', her attitudes in danger of hardening into blinkered self-satisfaction.

Meanwhile, 'Paul began'. A high-spirited man who 'went like steel to magnet for the essence of any person, place, activity or situation, working from no preconception or preferred framework,' Paul was an Oxford undergraduate who came to the family house to tutor Athill's younger brother. At fifteen, Diana fell fervently in love – with the man, and with his embrace of life – and, in that moment, 'the lines of my life were laid down'. She learned, through her irrepressibly open-minded lover, to regard difference without prejudice, to move between worlds, even bring them together. It was Paul, Athill tells us, who 'broke down my conditioning and made me anxious to meet people as people, regardless of class or race: a freedom from shackles which did not then chafe me, but which would probably have become locked on me, for which I shall always thank him.'

The social breadth of this new vision was matched by an intense sensuality that intoxicated Diana.

> When [Paul] went with me to pick primroses one Easter . . . he was astonished at my matter-of-fact attitude to the thick cushions of flowers in a certain part of the wood. I took it for granted that primroses grew thickly there – they always did. He, who lived either in London or on the coast, where they did not flourish, *saw* them.

Paul buried his face in a clump of primroses, laughing. After that, Diana *saw:*

> At once the frail, reddish, slightly hairy stalks of the primroses, their delicate petals, the neat funnels of their centres, the young leaves, folded and lettuce-green among the darker, broader old ones, the grouping of each constellation of flowers, their delicious, rain-fresh scent – everything about them became alive.

In the mid-1930s, Athill went up to Oxford to study English Literature. During her three years there, she became engaged to Paul, at the same time enjoying sundry 'subsidiary relationships' with other men: 'little explosions of meeting' that 'were constantly blasting new shafts into the mine of experience.' She and her friends lived in the shadow of impending war, but managed to be happy, to avoid feeling blighted by 'this horror about life'. 'I was frivolous, and I was lazy,' she says of her undergraduate self, 'and it seems to me now that I was lucky to be those things, because by being able almost all the time to slide sideways, not to think, I could store three years away like jewels before it came.'

The horror, when 'it' hit, came not only in the form of the Second World War and its bombs. In a cruelly protracted way, Diana lost Paul. The shock of this rejection tore a hole in her life, marking the start of what she refers to as 'twenty years of unhappiness'. Her contented childhood and her happy years at Oxford had given her a stability and resilience that ultimately helped her to retain her 'bias towards being *well-disposed* to life.' But for a long time, 'the most intense emotion [she] could conceive of was one of pain.'

Athill's account of the 'revolting humiliations' of grief and of the spartan emotional existence into which she sank during the war is pungent with sadness and haunted by a creeping threat of sourness. 'A long, flat unhappiness of that sort drains one, substitutes for blood some thin, acid fluid with a disagreeable smell,' she observes. 'Years of emptiness. Years leprous with boredom, drained by the war of meaning.' Having found a modest job working for the BBC's Overseas Service, she 'retreated into a curious hermit existence' while her 'soul shrank to the size of a pea.'

Athill analyses her misery – and her attempts to dodge or defeat it – with exquisite acuity. *Instead of a Letter* glitters with chiaruscuro effects, evincing the author's life-saving skill at seeing in the dark. 'After the late shift the tiny sequins of the traffic lights, reduced by masks during the blackout, changed from red to amber to green down the whole length of empty, silent Oxford Street. They looked as though they were signalling a whispered conversation, and they were the kind of thing with which I filled my days.'

To fill her nights as well as her days, Athill began to 'grab at emotion' in a series of 'foolish' and brief sexual encounters. In these harsher, sadder passages, *Instead of a Letter* is suffused with an unusual kind of intimacy. The narrative not only explores the recesses of Athill's psyche and 'the body's truth', revealing her most private thoughts, feelings and actions, but also invites the reader to watch the writer watching herself. 'I would split in two,' she says of her trance-like phase of casual affairs, 'one half going obediently and easily through the routine, the other watching with an ironic amusement.' The sharpness of what she elsewhere refers to as her 'beady eye' (trained, to such comic and discomfiting effect, upon others in her later memoirs) is here very often turned upon herself.

This 'watching half' of Athill keeps her work refreshingly free of self-absorption. Escaping the characteristic dangers of memoir, she reveals herself without sliding into narcissism, and lights up the smallest, most ordinary details of her life in a way that conveys their significance and appeal without distorting them through exaggeration or sentimentality. Hers is a rare kind of candour: she addresses her readers with a strikingly modern lack of squeamishness and secrecy about personal experience, but is never gratuitously shocking or cloyingly confessional. It is, as she acknowledges, 'difficult to consider with detachment' such experiences as promiscuity, abortion, and the life-threatening miscarriage she describes in *After a Funeral*. But Athill writes with a detachment that is carefully calibrated. Her memoirs have a distinctive introspective quality – free of claustrophobia, yet never less than fully engaged. Rendering her ordeals and delights, she pulls us into her story, her consciousness, without pushing us into the sticky position of voyeurs. She makes us privy to sometimes shocking intimacies but spares us the imposition of any self-pity. The depth of her psychological probing is matched and relieved by a tonic buoyancy in the telling.

Despite its frequent sadness, *Instead of a Letter* is a radiant and inspiring book. Its final episodes surge with a sense of revival as Athill describes how 'one by one, nerves which I thought to be dead have come to life.' It also reveals how she became a writer: the very moment, as so often in her work, brought to life.

One January morning in 1958: 'I was crossing the Outer Circle in Regent's Park, bringing my dog in from her walk, when a passing car slowed, accelerated again, slowed and stopped.' A comic moment of misrecognized identity and mistaken assumptions followed, leaving Athill feeling 'extraordinarily alive and cheerful'. As soon as she got home, she began to jot down memories inspired by her brief encounter with the man in the car. 'At that point it happened': propelled by 'the energy, the feeling of something bubbling inside me,' her first story 'came straight out, with no pause.'

Beyond her commitment 'to get it *just as it was*', and a determination to write a story that she 'meant people to read', Athill had no clearly defined sense of her literary enterprise. She distinguished between 'invented' stories and those that corresponded more closely to her own experience, but made no sharper distinction between fiction and non-fiction, except to observe that, although she felt prouder of the 'invented' stories, the others were usually better.

*Instead of a Letter* began as an impromptu experiment. Looking back (forty years later) on the genesis of her first book, Athill remembered:

> I put a piece of paper in my typewriter and began to write – about my grandmother! And from there it went on – this is literally true – without my ever knowing when I sat down to write what I was going to say. I would be dying to say it, whatever it was – really itching to get back to the typewriter the moment I got home from the office (and sometimes scribbling away under my desk when I was in the office) – but I never knew what it was going to be.

The editor-turned-author was, without realizing it, contributing to the birth of a new kind of literature. Memoir has grown to be a popular genre, unveiling lives whose richness lurks in private moments rather than public achievement. But in the late 1950s, when Athill began to write, there was no obvious and welcoming category to contain what she was saying and how she was saying it. She expressed herself with a literary and emotional openness that was remarkable for its time – and helps to account for the enduring freshness of her writing.

In this uncannily still-vivid book, Athill offers – lightly, generously – a kaleidoscope of meditations on love, sex and rejection, on pain, humiliation and loss, on aloneness and friendship and faith,

Englishness, class and race. Her thoughts are often ebullient with wit, always marked by a passionate push towards personal and social honesty, a commitment 'to understand, to be aware, to touch the truth'. *Instead of a Letter* shows us how a person can save herself by 'seeing things', keeping her eyes open and on the world.

Andrea Ashworth

# 1

MY MATERNAL GRANDMOTHER died of old age, a long and painful process. Heart and arteries began to show signs of wearing out when she was ninety-two years old, but it was not until two years later that they failed her and precipitated her – still lucid, still herself – into death. By the end, pain and exhaustion had loosened her grip on life so that when she 'recovered' yet again from a heart attack she would whisper, 'Why doesn't God let me die?' but for a long time she was afraid of what was happening to her. She was afraid of death, and she was sorrowful – which was worse – because she had much time in which to ask herself what her life had been for, and often she could not answer.

I was not much with her at that time. Her son and her daughters, who lived near or with her, laboured through it at her side, but her grandchildren were scattered and saw her only when they visited their parents. But once I happened to be there when she was very ill and everyone was more than usually worn out, so I took a night watch. I sat in her cold room (if the windows were shut she felt suffocated), watching the dark hollows of her eyes and the shocking dark hole of her mouth – it was unbearable that Gran, always so completely in control of appearances, should lie with her mouth agape. I listened to the rhythm of her breathing. Sometimes it would stop for a whole minute and the winter night would be absolutely still. In the long silences I prayed to her God, 'Please, please don't let her start breathing again,' and knew that if she died it would not be frightening, that I should feel peace. But each time the harsh, snoring breaths would begin again, hauling her back to another awakening and to more pain and physical humiliation. It was some weeks after that, when she had rallied to the extent of writing an angry letter to the local paper about a new road of which she disapproved, and of ordering a dentist to her bedside to make her a new set of false teeth, that she turned her beautiful speckled eyes towards me one afternoon and said in so many words: 'What have I lived for?'

It was she who should have been able to tell me that. All her life she had been a churchgoing Christian of apparently unshaken faith. But she was on her own then: not suffering, like Doctor Johnson, from fear of the consequences of her sinfulness according to the teachings of that faith, but simply unsupported by it. I said to her what I believed: that she had lived, at the very least, for what her life had been. The long, hard months of dying could eclipse her life, but they did not expunge it. What she had created for us, her family, by loving and being loved, still existed, would continue to exist, and could not have existed without her. 'Do you really think that it has been worth something?' she asked, and I held her hands and told her that I believed it with all my heart. Then I went away, and wondered. For her it might well be the truth. She had created a world for us. Even if I had been the only one of her descendants to have been rooted in that world (and perhaps I was one of the least deeply rooted of them all), something that her love had made would still be alive. But what of a woman who had never had the chance, or had missed the chance, to create something like that? What of myself? That was a question to whistle up an icy wind, and I was out in it. I waited for the shivering to start.

Well, it has not started yet, and I would like to know why. Which is my reason for sitting down to write this.

# 2

I T IS STRANGE to have loved someone like my grandmother, with whom I came to disagree on almost everything of importance. In anyone but her the values she held seem to me absurd or shocking, yet there she is: the dominant figure in my curiously matriarchal family, her memory warm with love, pleasure, and gratitude.

When she was a girl, one of four handsome daughters of a Master of an Oxford college, she swore that she would never be kissed by any man but the one she would marry, and she never was. She met her husband when he was an undergraduate: a man with frosty blue eyes and a trace of Yorkshire accent ('cassel' for castle, 'larndry' for laundry), who read for the bar but did not practise for long because he inherited his father's estate, which I shall call Beckton. It was not in Yorkshire but in East Anglia, to which his family had moved because his mother was supposed to be delicate and to need a softer climate. She must in fact have been a hardy woman in spite of delicate looks, for she lived to a good age, and if the climate of East Anglia is softer than that of Yorkshire, heaven forbid that I should ever have to winter in the latter.

My grandmother bore her husband four daughters, of whom my mother was the youngest; and at last, when I suspect that a sense of failure was beginning to prey on her, one son. She despised women, or thought that she did. Intelligent herself, happy to send two of her girls to Oxford when it was still uncommon, and proud of any success her female grandchildren might achieve in unwomanly careers, she yet insisted that women's minds were inferior to men's. There was some kind of ambiguity at work here, for although masculine superiority was never questioned, the climate of my grandmother's house was markedly feminine and her daughters' husbands always seemed to be slightly on the fringe of it. On a subject suitable to men – war, politics, a question of local government, the appointment of a clergyman to a living – she would turn to a son-in-law with a formal deference: 'I have been wanting to ask you – ought I to write to the bishop . . .?' but if she intended to write to the bishop, that was what she would do, whatever the son-in-law said. It was not that the deference was false, but perhaps it was paid to a figure too masculine, too infallible to exist: a pattern of manhood to which the real men in the family failed wholly to conform.

Whether my grandfather conformed to it or not I do not know, for he died when I was six. If he did not, it was through no fault of his wife's. All I know of their relationship is that their two writing-desks in the library at Beckton Manor were so placed that his was near the fire and hers far from it, and that when, after his death, she referred to him it was always as though he were unquestionable in whatever he said or did. The references were infrequent, but they followed a pattern: 'Grandpapa always said . . .' and so it was; 'Grandpapa would never let the children . . .' and so they never did; 'Grandpapa was very fond of . . .' and so it was good. That she had adored him was an article of faith in the family, but during her last illness she disconcerted one of her daughters. They were talking of her fear of death. 'I don't understand why you are so afraid,' said her daughter. 'You have always been religious – surely you believe in an afterlife and that you will meet Dad again?' My grandmother, it seems, said nothing. 'But,' I was told, 'she gave me such a *very odd* look, it quite shocked me.' The look may have referred to the afterlife in general, but her daughter had an uncomfortable feeling that it referred to Grandpapa.

What do I know about him? That he had blunt, North Country good looks; that he had discriminating taste in silver and wine and built up a large and excellent library with its emphasis on history; that when he enlarged Beckton Manor, making it U-shaped instead of L-shaped, he set up a kiln to make small bricks matching those of the house, which was built in about 1760, and employed skilled workmen to carve stone to a Georgian design round his new front door and to mould plaster swags to crown the Adams chimney-piece he put in his new drawing room. A man of taste, but backward-looking. He would give sixpences to his children for learning *Lycidas* before they were eight, wrote in well managed Johnsonian cadences a thesis on the Serbs (whom he called Servs), and travelled modestly in Italy and Greece, bringing back stone urns for the terrace wall and insisting that his accompanying children put permanganate in the foreign water with which they had to brush their teeth. He was a good farmer. The estate at Beckton is of a thousand acres, some of the land rented out to tenants but much of it attached to the Manor Farm. My grandfather employed a bailiff from Yorkshire, but he took most of the management on himself and did it well.

I cannot recall any word spoken to me by my grandfather. His children's talk of him has always been as unquestioning as his widow's, and sometimes affectionate. He was not quite a tyrant, perhaps, but they convey that he ruled his roost as though by divine right, and I do not think that I would have liked him. Death lent him a sort of holiness for a time. His soul flew out of open sash windows and 'went to Heaven to be with God', which gave him a share of God's benevolence. After that he did a miracle for me, permitting me to walk unstung through a bed of nettles. Each spring, when we made cowslip balls for my grandmother's birthday, we put the best of them on his grave, an austere grey slab with the words 'Tomorrow to fresh woods and pastures new' carved on it, but the feeling of piety and love which attended this tribute was engendered by the act rather than directed towards the memory of a real man. And the things I owe him – Beckton as a place in which to grow up, books as an indispensable part of life – soon came to seem Gran's dispensation, not his.

She went on being there. After breakfast she would put on an

overall and brush the dogs out on the terrace by the steps which led
into the library. Wearing thick leather gloves she would garden in
her greenhouse, or the rose beds, would cut flowers for the house
and would arrange them in the 'flower room', where the vases were
kept and where the dogs slept. She wrote many letters on small
sheets of black-edged paper, in writing so like shorthand that only
her daughters knew the secret of reading it. She went for a long
walk every day and took a strong dose of senna pods every night:
fresh air and open bowels were, she considered, all that was
necessary for health. Her housekeeping, to which she paid vigilant
attention, was simplified by custom. Vegetables, milk, eggs, and
butter all came from the estate; hams were cured, honey was
harvested, or jam was made at fixed times, and the groceries were
ordered by post every month, from the Civil Service Stores in
London. It was a simple, rhythmical life in which she was only
concerned with the management, not the execution, but when
much later she moved to a smaller house and staff problems
combined with the dwindling of a fixed income forced her to do
things herself, she knew how to clean, dust, polish silver, and so on
much better than the rest of us, who had been doing it for years as
a matter of course.

The pleasures of her life were the place itself, which she adored,
her family, and reading: her existence should have been a tranquil
one. What was it that made anxiety such a distinct thread in it?
Never could anyone go away from Beckton without my
grandmother's eyes expressing real unhappiness. The journey
might be a short one, made for pleasure, but she still felt a clutch
of fear. We were not going to eat enough, and what we ate would
be unwholesome; we were going to sleep with our windows shut;
we were going to catch some infectious disease; a car was going to
skid or a train run off the rails. Bad things were likely to happen to
people if they went away. I have noticed this attitude in other people
whose lives are secure, comfortable, and sheltered by privilege so
that one would expect disaster to be far from their minds. I
suppose, whether they recognize it or not, it is an acknowledgment
of the forces besieging their position. My grandmother had a good

knowledge of history and read *The Times* daily: she knew what was happening in the world. Wars and rumours of war; communists abroad and socialists at home; rising taxes and falling respect for tradition. She, a conservative, a gentlewoman, a devout Protestant Christian and an owner of property, was automatically on the defensive against powers outside her control. She did not trust 'outside' and converted her distrust into fear of accident and careless eating. Over and over again I have heard her, or someone like her, say in a voice of real dismay, 'But you can't go on that train, you'll miss lunch!' as though they had become obsessed by the value of food because of some experience of hardship or starvation. In their time measured out not by coffee spoons but by dishes of roast beef, steak-and-kidney puddings, apple pie and cream, they have never once felt or expected to feel a pang of true hunger, so from where does this irrational panic come if it is not a symbol of something else?

My grandmother's anxiety increased as she grew older, because she felt that the right, the natural order of things would be for her to be able to provide for us all on her death, and it was clear that she could not do so; but when I was a child it was less explicit. It was simply darling Gran fussing, and if you teased her about it she smiled back ruefully, half amused by herself, half expressing 'It is all very well for you to laugh, if only you knew.'

My father had a family, but it did not own Beckton. It owned no land at all. My paternal grandfather, a clergyman in comfortable circumstances, shot himself for no good reason while I was still a baby (the coal had not been delivered on time, I believe: he had high blood pressure and would therefore fly into violent rages over small matters). It was as 'good' a family as my mother's and although it had left East Anglia long ago, it had a better claim than hers on our own beloved county, having several tombs and brasses there to prove the existence of rustic Athill knights and one fishmonger at a respectable distance in time. In spite of this my mother felt it to be a family inferior to hers, and somehow, I can no longer remember exactly in what way, conveyed this idea to her children. She always felt that possession by her was nine-tenths of anything's value, even a dog's. A woman who loved animals to the point of absurdity, she rarely admitted charm or breeding in a dog belonging to someone else. 'It's not a bad-looking puppy, I suppose,' she would say, 'but it's going to be leggy' – or, 'One of those hysterical dogs, always ready to make a fuss of strangers.' In the same way, her husband's family bored and irritated her. It was as though when they were first married and conflicting loyalties emerged – with whom, for instance, should they spend Christmas? – she had said like a child 'Bags I my family,' and had got away with it ever since.

Because of Beckton, this was easy to do. A house with twenty bedrooms, standing in a large garden and park with a thousand acres of land round it, can absorb children far more easily than can a neat six-bedroomed house with a two-acre garden, like that of my paternal grandmother, who lived in Devonshire. It was more *sensible* to go to Beckton for the holidays. And if we or any of our cousins had been ill, or our parents were abroad, Beckton Gran could house us with much pleasure and little inconvenience, while Devonshire Grannie, fond though she was of us, would have had to turn her house upside down. Besides, my father was an Army offcer with, during all my childhood, the rank of major, and with private means so small that they hardly counted. He lived above his income, modestly and anxiously, from the day he was married, but even by doing that he could not afford to give his wife and children so good a time as they had at Beckton: he would have felt churlish had he prevented their visits. I doubt, indeed, whether he could have done so if he had tried. My mother was strong-willed and he had the disadvantage of being the one *qui aimait*. So although I and my younger brother and sister knew that our official home was where he happened to be working – Woolwich, or when he retired from the Army and took a job in the city, Hertfordshire – our 'real' home, the place to which we 'came home' from other places, was Beckton.

Having bought a small glass bottle made in about 1785, club-shaped, with a delicate spiral rib from neck to base, I was looking at it with affection, enjoying the colour of the glass and the hint of irregularity in the shape. Why, I began to wonder, are objects made in England during that period so much my home territory when it comes to aesthetic pleasure? The products of other centuries and of other countries I have learnt to appreciate, but I cannot remember having to *learn* to delight in those of the English eighteenth century. Probably, I concluded, it is because so much of my upbringing took place in an eighteenth-century house. It was a thought with gratifying implications. I am glad that I have not inherited money or possessions, and I *would* be glad if I could be sure that I had not inherited any prejudices or attitudes of mind towards other people, but I liked the idea of a child's mind and eye unconsciously trained by graceful shapes, just proportions, and the details of good craftsmanship. It suggested that whatever faults the middling English gentry might have, they would be likely to possess a certain feeling for grace and style: good for us!

Then, unfortunately, I began to remember various objects bought by my relatives, prized by them and admired by myself before I left home and began to sniff round museums and listen to the opinions of people better educated in such matters than myself. I remembered certain lamps and pieces of china and materials for curtains or chair covers . . . It was true that we were all familiar with one kind of beauty so that if any of us became interested in aesthetics, that kind, being familiar, would be easy to start with; but it was clearly not true that we had gained from it any ingrained, generally applicable sense of quality or style. If the inhabitants of Beckton had to buy something new and were unable to afford to go to the right place for it (the family's fortunes have been coasting downhill all my life), choice would be conditioned not by knowledge, but by familiarity. The new object would be a pitiful, decadent bastard of the old and we would be cheerfully blind to the difference between patina and French polish, cut glass and moulded, a graceful curve and a clumsy one. Only a few members of my family had, if left to themselves, more natural taste than the people they most pitied and despised: the dwellers in suburbia. (The working classes were allowed a few distinct and even endearing merits: suburbanites – no!)

New purchases were not often made, partly because everything in Beckton Manor was certainly 'good' in the sense of being solid and enduring, partly because, even early in my lifetime, extravagance was condemned. It was still a rich man's house compared to those of the vast majority, but the family did not feel itself a rich family. There was a strict line drawn between necessities and luxuries, and luxuries were suspect.

During my early childhood, necessities included a head gardener with two men under him, two grooms, a chauffeur, a butler and a footman, a cook and a kitchenmaid with a scullery maid to help them, a head housemaid with two under-housemaids, and my grandmother's lady's maid. They included, too, animals for our pleasure and governesses and schools for our instruction. They included books, and a great deal of wholesome food, linen sheets rather than cotton, and three separate rooms for being in at different times ofthe day, not counting the dining-room, the smoking-room, the front hall, in which, for some reason, my grandmother always had tea, and the nursery. Capital being inviolate, there can, indeed, have been little income left over after the maintenance of all this at what was felt to be its proper level.

Clothes for my mother's generation and then for us were almost all made at home or in the village, except for the obligatory coat and skirt, and riding clothes, for which we went to a good tailor. My mother, happily for me, was the extravagant one of the family. She used to make gleeful and guilty forays to London for clothes, but it was an adventure, not routine. My grandfather had travelled a little (since it was before I can remember, I see it as Making the Grand Tour), but after his death it was unusual for anyone to take a holiday abroad, while to buy curtains for your bedroom simply because you were tired of the old ones was unheard of. If the old ones fell to pieces so that you *had* to replace them, you only considered the cheaper ranges of material (even my mother never considered the *most* expensive), and then – alas for that instinctive taste which, for a moment, I attributed to us. If you liked pink roses you chose pink roses, regardless of how the rest of the room was furnished. Sometimes you would recognize aesthetics to the point of saying 'The blue in the pattern picks up the blue in the carpet,' indicating a tiny blue motif in the design which, if examined closely, could be seen almost to match an equally inconspicuous blue twirl in the carpet's pattern; or sometimes you would speak the words which have sealed the fate of so many British interiors, and of the appearances of so many Englishwomen: 'It is a good colour because *it goes with anything*.'

Yet Beckton Manor was a charming house to be in, and so are almost all the English houses of its kind that I have known. Like its fellows, it had plenty of lovely things in it by chances of inheritance or the good taste of individuals, and it had something else as well. Its inhabitants might not be interested in decoration, but they were interested in nature: to flowers, trees, skies, landscapes and weather they responded with a strong sense of beauty, and without thinking of it they brought into the house as much of nature as they could. The tables loaded with cut flowers, the flowery chintzes, the indifferent watercolours of beloved places expressed the life lived from the house, and they pleased.

As a child, of course, I thought it not only lovely but inevitable: that was what a house should be. Any house which did not have those things in it, and which did not look out over terrace and park to a lake beyond which rose the Lake Covert (landscaped by Capability Brown, we all mistakenly believed), was only a poor attempt at a house. When my mother scolded me for bragging to a friend of the number of bedrooms at Beckton and the two islands in the lake, telling me that one should never show off about good fortune to those with less, she may have improved my manners but she did not diminish my sense of superiority. Even the cold was a matter of pride. Warmth did not rate as a necessity, since it was held to be the opposite of fresh air and therefore unhealthy, so everyone was crippled by chilblains from November to February. 'My sponge is *often* frozen solid in the morning,' I remember boasting to some less hardy, less fortunate child.

How guilty do I feel at having come in on the tail end of such a life and having loved so passionately a place founded on privilege the earning of which had become remote? I do not often refer to it, and when I think about it a figure appears opposite me: that of some faceless friend brought up in a Manchester back street, with a childhood very different from my own stored in his head. At his most charitable, I feel, he would be giving me a quizzical look; and if I were to repeat to him the kind of thing my grandmother, my parents, my other relatives of their generation and even some of my own would say about his accent, his clothes, his attitudes . . . Well, how could I repeat that kind of thing? And if he were a Jew or a Negro, or some other kind of foreigner not of noble birth (for a foreigner can only be guaranteed a gentleman by a title), then what could he feel towards my background less than disgust?

That smug, matter-of-fact assumption of superiority! Many landed families were richer and better bred than mine; nuances which mine recognized but which made no difference to their certainty. Except when it came to lords, whose acquaintance gave them a pleasure verging on the undignified, they were convinced that they were the best kind of people to be (indeed there was something a little fishy about anyone not a lord who was richer or grander than they were). When my grandparents dismissed someone as 'not a gentleman', their unthinking certainty had the force of a *moral judgment*; while the tinge of apology or defiance that crept into the same judgment when pronounced by my parents' generation was only faint.

This attitude was at the best comic, at the worst repulsive, for with what could that particular family support its certainty of being 'the best'? The abilities of most of its members were respectable but ordinary, their achievements no more than commonplace. None of them was unusually intelligent or energetic and most of them lacked imagination to a remarkable degree. Generous and affectionate they could be, but they hardly ever extended these qualities outside the family circle. Like anyone else they had their charms, their interesting quirks, their endearing or impressive aspects, and their standard of behaviour was, within certain limits, civilized and reliable, but it was not just in matters of taste that they were no better than anyone else: physically, intellectually, and morally they were no more than middling. Yet they despised almost all the rest of the world, excepting people as nearly as possible replicas of themselves, as though their status as English country gentlefolk made them exceptional beings; something of which they fell short even by their own standards, for they were not well enough connected, and Beckton was not a large enough estate, for them to come anywhere near the top of the ladder of snobbery.

What made my family so profoundly self-satisfied? That question has puzzled me more with every year of my life. The satisfaction in itself was not objectionable, since people can only function comfortably if they have it; but its obverse – the disdain or distrust of anyone not of their kind – that was stupid, ugly, and pitiful, and it is a curious sensation to be bound by enduring ties of love and habit to a set of people who so stubbornly displayed it. All that money spent on education, and so little thinking done as a result of it! Reactions still triggered by the sound of a vowel, the cut of a coat, the turn of a phrase . . . 'He was wearing what I think he would have called a *sports jacket*,' said one of them, only the other day (he would have called it a tweed coat), and that, as far as the wearer of the sports jacket was concerned, was that. Once imbued with such reactions, it is impossible entirely to escape them: I know that until the day I die I shall be unable to avoid *noticing* 'raound' for 'round', 'involave' for 'involve' (on that one an Army officer of my acquaintance used to turn down candidates for a commission), because a built-in mechanism will always click, however much I dislike it, 'placing' everyone I meet as though for a second it was my parents eyes and ears at work, not mine. But once it has clicked it can very easily be disregarded. The puzzle lies in the choice not to disregard it.

An old man near death once gave my uncle great pleasure by telling him that a treasured memory – something which had remained for years in his mind as a vignette of the England he loved – had been a glimpse, once caught as he was driving by, of my uncle riding in the park at Beckton. It is a pretty park, well planted with groups of beech and oak trees, sloping gracefully down to the lake beyond which the wood known as the Lake

Covert rises, and mildly dominated by the house (to the left of the picture as the old man approached it), standing on its balustraded terrace with a great cedar tree at one corner of it to break its slightly austere Georgian lines. 'It was a perfect October afternoon,' said the old man. 'There was the Lake Covert, all golden in its autumn leaves, reflected in the water, and there were you, cantering along beside the lake on that black of yours – what a beautiful horse he was – with a couple of dogs running behind you. I watched you and I thought, Now that's a lovely scene, that's England, and I've never forgotten it.'

Describing the conversation, and the old man's emotion my uncle gave a slight deprecating laugh, but he was not only touched, he was satisfied. That man had recognized in him and his setting what he himself felt deeply to be their true nature, and as he savoured it he was likable rather than absurd. He was moved by a vision of something which he dearly loved and which had comforted him when, during the war, he was badly wounded: he felt genuinely that it was worth dying for. To have said to him, 'But you are not England. You and what you represent are only a tiny fraction of England and an archaic one at that, preserved not by deeds or virtue but by money most of which you yourself do not earn' – to have said that would have been to have attacked not a fancy but a rooted belief. He might have answered, 'All right, so it is preserved by money: money in the hands of the right people, of people like us. What further argument do you need for the existence of such people and such money?' He and his like have been snug all their lives, and snugness breeds smugness – but smugness is too small a word for what it feels like *from inside*. From inside, it feels like moral and aesthetic *rightness*; from inside, it is people like me, who question it, who look stupid, ugly, and pitiful – and ungrateful, too. Why admit that the grammar-school boy, the self-made businessman, the artist, the foreigner or whatever are just as likely to be 'the best' as we are, when such an admission must attack certainty, the cosiest of all the gifts bestowed by privilege? It is not only ingratitude, it is treachery.

Treacherous I may be, but ungrateful I am not. I consider it good fortune to have been born of Beckton's youngest daughter, not of its son, at a point in time and a position in the family where diminishing resources had brought unthinking certainty up against the facts of life and worn it comparatively thin. Never to have broken through its smothering folds would have been, I have always thought, extremely depressing. But on the other hand, not to have enjoyed a childhood wrapped warmly in those folds – that would be a sad loss. There I used to be, as snug and as smug as anyone, believing with the best that we were the best – and if security is the thing for children, which it surely is, then how lucky I was.

Beckton and Gran: they blur together. When I think of her I may see a handsome woman with crisp, pure-white hair (it turned when she was thirty), wearing a black, black-and-white, or grey dress with a crossover bodice and a lace collar (she was in her eighties before she forgot her widow's status to the point of wearing a dress made of soft, pinky-red wool). Her eyes, with lids that droop slightly in an odd way at the outer corners, are speckled green and grey, capable of an ironic expression but usually full of affection, and she will be looking at me attentively, ready to be amused or interested by what I am saying (for one did not say to Gran the things which would have shocked or displeased her). I may see this woman, or I may think of getting out of the car to open the white gate between park and lawn, breathing that first, almost drinkable, smell of grass, flowers, and cedar tree which was the assurance that we were home. Then images come crowding in: the stream in the kitchen garden in which the newts and tadpoles lived; the marble children under a tree on the library chimneypiece; the scalloped black-green leather which would pull off from the edges of the nursery bookshelves; the goat-shed in the lower stable yard made into a bower of beech branches by a cousin and myself, because tender young beech leaves on the branch were what our goats liked best (we gave them senna pods, too, when we thought they needed them, and sometimes an aspirin or a spoonful of cough linctus). Very clear is the chasm between the back of the sofa and the bookshelves in the morning room, where I would squat for hours to read bound volumes of *Punch*, and the smell of the plush curtains over the double door between morning

room and front hall, in which I had only to muffle myself, at one
time, in order to begin writing a play in which a cousin was to take
the part of a good, blond and slightly insipid princess while I was to
be the dark, wicked one, like Sir Rider Haggard's She-Who-Must-
Be-Obeyed. 'Go and play in the morning room, darlings,' people
would say. It was the room to which children graduated from the
nursery, where one could bounce on the furniture or litter the floor
with Meccano or cutting-out.

There was only one unpleasant thing in that house: the ghost in
the night nursery, where at our smallest we usually had to sleep. It
was not an ordinary ghost but a disgusting presence, a slimy grey
thing like a stubby elephant's trunk which reached down over the
gutter and groped at the window one morning while I was sitting
alone on my pot. No one liked that room, which was at the back of
the house, looking out on to a gloomy thicket of yew trees, on the
old principle, not otherwise observed, of pushing children out of
the way with the servants. But no one thought of telling my
grandmother about that, so it was nothing to do with her. Every
other sound, smell, and texture in the place I loved quite
consciously from the earliest time I can remember, and I loved it so
much not only because I felt it to be beautiful, but because its
presiding genius, my grandmother, loved me.

In relationships outside her family she was not a loving woman,
nor a tolerant one. Her servants she distrusted, not (the older, long-
established ones anyway) in terms of honesty so much as of sense.
She expected them to be ninnies, and to be dirty, and how they
managed not to be the latter is hard to see, considering that it was
years before anyone thought of putting in a bathroom on the attic
floor where they lived, while they were not allowed to use ours. Of
people who differed from her on politics or religion she was fiercely
scornful, particularly of anyone who believed that the Pope spoke
God's word, or who was a socialist. Of foreigners she was not only
scornful, but distrustful as well. If they thought that they could
govern their own countries better than we could she considered
them both fools and traitors. Outside the ramifications of what
might be called the greater family as opposed to the central family –

the second cousins and so on, about whose fortunes she was always completely and mysteriously informed and whom she wished well – she had no intimate friends.

Described like this, she sounds a disagreeable woman, yet no one ever met her without being charmed. The charm came from the warmth of her personality, and the warmth came from the dynamo of love at work in her for the benefit of her children and her children's children. She was not soft with them. She mocked them if their politics veered to the left, scolded them if they did not eat properly, and criticized any folly they might get up to unless it was something really grave, like marrying a foreigner or having an extra-marital love affair. About that kind of thing she would either keep silent, or would choose not to know. But although her family could cause her impatience or grief, they could not diminish her love – and the only grief they could have caused her when still young would have been by illness or death. In her house we could be excited by our own misdemeanours, but we could never feel that they put us in peril, so for us this autocratic woman, whose sharp intelligence was deliberately confined to so narrow a range, created a benign air which we could always breathe again, even in middle age, simply by going back to the place where she lived.

I shocked her once. I was about ten years old and had thought of an image for life. I thought that it was as though people were confined in a bowl which was floating on a sea. While snug at the bottom of the bowl they lived their lives complacently, but the bowl spun and tossed on the sea and its spinning sometimes sent one of them up its side until he could see over the rim. All round would be the endless chaos of dangerous, cold grey water, unsuspected till then, and anyone who had seen it and had understood that what he had thought was safety was only a little bowl, would not be able to bear it. That, I decided, was the origin of madness. I was proud of this idea, described it to my grandmother, and was disconcerted to see her so upset. It was not at all clever, she said sharply, to think that life was aimless, and she told me to remember the then Prince of Wales, who had recently made some statement of high purpose and idealism to a gathering of Boy Scouts.

I was disappointed by this response, which did not seem to me
to recognize the implications of my idea, but I remember it because
in spite of my disappointment, its inadequacy did not matter. I
noted that in some ways I would have to differ from Gran but I did
not feel betrayed, because there she was as she spoke, wearing the
kind of dress she always wore, with her beautiful hair and her dear,
kind eyes watching me with the anxiety I thought was a joke and
the love which I would never think of questioning. I myself might
incline more to the bowl theory than the Prince of Wales theory,
but clearly whatever Gran believed was *good*, because it was
believed by Gran.

# 3

I FELT OUTRAGED when someone first pointed out to me that my
grandmother's house was not 'mine'. When she died, or decided
to make way for my uncle, it would be his, and then his son's, or,
if he had no son, his daughter's. Supposing he had no children, I
asked hopefully (he was still unmarried at the time). Working on
the assumption that succession to the estate would follow the
pattern established by the monarchy, it appeared that at least twelve
people, seven of them my contemporaries, would have to die before
I would have a claim, and I hardly felt I ought to pray for this
however much I would have liked to.

Perhaps this realization came near the time when I lay sprawled
on short grass in the back park one spring morning – there were
lambs about, and daisies – facing the knowledge that in three years'
time I would be thirteen. What made the passage of so long a
stretch of time real to me I cannot remember, but it was appalling,
giving me a horrible sensation as though my insides had gone cold
and empty. To be in my teens, I saw suddenly, would be to leave
childhood behind, to be in a world where impossible things could
happen. I would become able to believe that the place would go to
my uncle; I would become able to foresee a time when, perhaps, I
could no longer return to it as though it were my home. Where
would my home be? Some place like those in which I had already
lived with my parents and brother and sister; a house and garden
just big enough for us, with none of our past worked into it and no

territory round it to call our own. Already, when we rode across country from the house my parents rented in Hertfordshire, we had to *ask permission* from the owners of the land, which had seemed to me humiliating. And the business of earning my living – it would not be something my father talked about when he was feeling pompous ('You will have to earn your living one day'), but something I should have *to do*. I do not think that I was shocked by the prospect; only frightened. It would surely be difficult and disagreeable, and, because the norm of existence was life at Beckton, it would be unnatural.

In fact, my grandmother went on living in the house until the beginning of the war, when I was twenty-two; it was fully there to go back to. But whoever had given me that early, painful glimpse of the truth had done me a good turn. From that time my love of Beckton began, slowly, to take a wistful, nostalgic turn: I felt that I must treasure every detail of it against the future, and I remember standing under the great beech tree by the lawn, trying to will some essence of myself into the still green air so that after I was dead my ghost would materialize there. But at the same time my fear of what would follow began, with acceptance of mutability, to rub away and other things entering my life increased in value. That particular bowl, it seemed, spun on no grey sea. It would be sad to be pushed over the rim, but what surrounded it was a landscape, and the landscape, as it became increasingly real, began to look interesting.

My fear of 'thirteen' had been prophetic, all the same, for I believe I had reached that age when my mother told me that we had 'lost our money'. What really happened was that, having lived above their income for too long, my parents were at last rapped over the knuckles by their bank. We were in the Hertfordshire house at the time, my father having retired from the Army to avoid transporting his reluctant family to India, and taken a job in the City with a firm connected with the mining of mica. Our house was called The Cottage, but it had six bedrooms and was staffed with Margaret, the cook; Violet, her sister, who was not exactly a nanny but looked after the children; Ursula, the governess; Doris, the housemaid;

Mrs Knight, who 'came in', and deaf Gatwood, full-time gardener. My parents felt that they were living austerely because we ourselves looked after our ponies and they had not kept on their own hunters, nor did they indulge in any luxuries. My mother had no fur coat and no jewels except a couple of mediocre diamond rings and the string of small pearls given her as a wedding present by her father. There was rarely any drink in the house beyond a bottle of sherry, and the furniture was a job lot of stuff, none of it valuable or beautiful and some of it as utilitarian as the hospital beds inherited from a convalescent home for officers run by a great-aunt during the 1914–18 war. According to their lights, my father and mother were not extravagant people, but still the bank said that unless they followed a certain clearly defined plan they might not cash any more cheques.

My mother did not take this with any enduring seriousness, being a practical and energetic woman with no objection to doing things for herself, and having the comfortable feeling that Beckton was still there in the background. She broke the news to me, however, with an almost dramatic gravity – she always had an appetite for 'the worst' – so that I was impressed.

'Are we really *poor*?' I asked.

'Yes, darling, I'm afraid so.'

'Will Violet have to go? And Ursie?'

'Yes, I expect you will go to school.'

Doris, Margaret, and Mrs Knight went too, and we had to make our own beds and dust the bedrooms. As my mother said soon afterwards, 'the really *bloody* thing about being poor is that if you leave something on the floor when you go out, you know that it *will still be there* when you get back'. At that time I was exchanging two letters a term with a boy I had been in love with since I was nine years old, and I must have described our plight because I remember a letter of his beginning, 'Dear Diana, I am sorry to hear that you are now poor.' I was touched by his delicacy in saying no more about it than that.

It was not long before Beckton came to the rescue. We were going to leave Hertfordshire and live at the Manor Farm, we were told, and to the children the whole thing instantly became a delight. My mother probably had other reasons for making the move, but to us it seemed merely the happy solution of the family's financial problems, and we were so pleased by it that it did not occur to us to worry about my father, who would continue to work in London and could not, therefore, live so far from it except at weekends. He took lodgings with the family of a man who had once been his own father's coachman, and bicycled to the station every day because my mother had to have the car. I suppose that we felt, vaguely, that it was horrid for him, but it was a relief not to have him in the house. My brother and I had worked out a formula by then: 'Mummy and Daddy are both very nice people, but they don't suit each other, they should never have got married' – this, perhaps, was borrowed from Ursula or Violet. They were quarrelling fiercely at the time, and it was a relief not to have to watch for signs of trouble and to know that if, at weekends, it came (as it usually did) it could only last for two days.

I always *liked* my father – he was a likeable man – but if I ever felt anything warmer than liking it was when I was so young that I cannot remember it. I did not consciously take my mother's side when they quarrelled (indeed, I often felt something like hatred for her irrational flares of temper, and considered that my father, not she, was in the right) – but in our nerves all three of us children were more sympathetic to her than we were to him. It was not until much later that I understood the trouble to come from the simple but deadly poison of physical incompatibility which my father did not feel and my mother had been too inexperienced to recognize during their courtship, but even as small children we could sense the nature of her irritability.

To be constantly loved and desired by someone whose touch is repulsive to you is a profound outrage. You may be in such a situation by your own fault or folly, but whatever the surface facts, you remain the situation's victim because the offence you are receiving goes beyond reason, into such deep recesses of your being. Feeling wicked for her reactions, my mother stubbornly and